About the Author

Litsa Nikolopoulou-Gogas was born in Aigion, a seaside town in the Northern Peloponnese in 1932, one of nine siblings. She migrated to Melbourne in 1957 on the S.S Tasmania. Married by arrangement to a fellow-immigrant, George Gogas, they had a daughter and two sons. They were blessed with ten grandchildren, but one of them, George, was tragically killed in a car accident at age nineteen, plunging his family into unspeakable pain.

Litsa always loved books and learning, but poverty and war in the forties prevented her from continuing with higher education. She became a dressmaker and in Australia worked as a machinist and later in milk bars. Despite the immense hardships with work and family obligations, she managed to write and publish, in Greek, seven books of poetry and prose all drawn from her lived experience in both Greece and Australia. Alongside the depiction of a hard life, there is also an innate optimism in all her books that the world will see better days.

While some of her work has appeared in English publications such as: *The Word is Round* (1983); *Harmony (*1991); *Re-Telling the Tale* (1994); *Here We Are* (1998) and *Mothers from the Edge* (2006), this is her first book-length work appearing in English translation from the original Greek, *Merikes Alithies* [Some Truths] in 2013.

This family photograph was taken in 1956 just before the author migrated to Australia. Litsa Nikolopoulou-Gogas in the back row, 4th from the left. Her sister, Ioanna Liakakou, is standing next to her.

Moments of Truth

Memories of Greece and Australia

Litsa Nikolopoulou-Gogas

Translated by Konstandina Dounis

ASPASIA

First published 2022 by Aspasia
a literary imprint of Australian Scholarly Publishing Pty Ltd
7 Lt Lothian St Nth, North Melbourne, Vic 3051

Tel: 03 9329 6963 / Fax: 03 9329 5452
enquiry@scholarly.info / www.scholarly.info

ISBN 978-1-922669-50-6

Cover design: Amelia Walker

Back cover photo: Costa Athanassiou

Dedicated to my grandson
George,
to our cherished boy
lost in a car accident at age nineteen

Mourning your youth
how did your light go out
withered like a lily
I lamented migration's sorrows
not realising the greater bitterness of death

Keep love in your heart. A life without it is like a sunless garden when the flowers are dead.

Oscar Wilde

Be glad of life because it gives you the chance to love, to work, to play and to look up at the stars.

Henry Van Dyke

The first step towards knowledge is to know that we are ignorant.

Lord David Cecil

Contents

Translator's Note

Litsa Nikolopoulou-Gogas' memoir, *Moments of Truth,* is a profoundly moving account of the events that informed and shaped her nearly nine-decade long life story: first, in her homeland, Greece, and then in her adopted homeland, Australia. In prose characterised by a sparseness of tone and searing honesty, she highlights the degree to which endemic patriarchy obliterated any dreams she might have harboured for determining her future choices; her fate was sealed at every turn. She writes with unflinching directness about her abuse as a little girl at the hands of a 'benevolent' uncle, of enforced migration due to the relentless poverty and debilitating dowry system, through to her enforced marriage in Australia in the name of honour and reputation.

Her narrative shines a spotlight on the simultaneous pain and allure inherent in a migrant's nostalgia for a far-away homeland, as well as about the complex relationship with the new country that becomes 'home', all of which is underscored by the vagaries of a working-class reality negotiating disparate cultures and languages. These perspectives frame those universal experiences common to us all: the joys and challenges of family life, the excitement of buying a home, the horror of loss.

Given my life-long preoccupation with bringing immigrant stories out of the shadows, it was incredibly satisfying translating this memoir from the original Greek (entitled *Merikes Alithies*, 2013) into English. It was also a difficult task. Capturing the tone and inherently elliptical quality of the original Greek was a formidable challenge. Moreover, I found the subject matter confronting, particularly the sections depicting childhood abuse, her frightening early experiences of being a promised bride, and the death of her grandson that decimated her very being. As always with my translations, I have eschewed the inclusion of explanatory notes, preferring instead to allow the power of the narrative to flow unencumbered.

Within my research into Greek-Australian women's literary writings, I have highlighted the degree to which these works collectively serve to 'fill in the blanks' in relation to post-war immigrant women's lived realities. Litsa Nikolopoulou-Gogas' *Moments of Truth* is a prime example of this. I am so pleased to have been able to render her story into the English language, thereby fulfilling her wish to bequeath it to her children and grandchildren in a language that they could fully understand and appreciate. However, there is more to it than that. This publication ensures that her story is made accessible to a new and wider readership generally.

May it travel well within the world-wide Greek Diaspora, within the wider Australian community, and within global networks where the writer's insistence on her right to tell her own story loudly and proudly could not have been more relevant or timely.

Dr Konstandina Dounis
Monash Education Academy,
Monash University
March 2021

Acknowledgements

Many people and experiences contribute to a book being written, people familiar, and unfamiliar, to us pass through our life, exerting their influence and our thoughts proceed. I thank them all. They all helped me in some way.

I thank my parents for giving me the gift of life and this fine gift that enables me to do what I do.

I thank my family who respects my endeavours.

I thank my sister, Ioanna, for many things. Where do I start? I can't find the words to thank her for her help in getting my work out there and for overseeing the publication of all my Greek-language books.

I thank Helen Nickas for encouraging me to publish my book in an English translation and for editing the final manuscript.

I thank Konstandina Dounis for her beautiful translation that makes it possible for my story to be read by my children and grandchildren and by English-speaking readers everywhere.

Prologue

So many years after having migrated to Australia where I live with the family I created, my son John, his wife Ann and their three sons, George (deceased), Nicholas and J.J., my daughter Helen, her husband Joe, and their four children, Bianca, Daniela, Joseph and Juliana, my son Peter, his wife Nicky, and their three children, Ben, Bethany and Dan, I am perpetually asked the same question at various gatherings. Namely, what was the reason that made me decide to leave my homeland and come to Australia, and if I'm happy with my life here in this second homeland.

This presents me with the opportunity to stress what we all know: the relentless poverty in our homeland was the main reason for our migration and there's no need for any further discussion on the matter. As for me personally, when I left my homeland I tried to cover everything with a misty veil, to stop time and events in that moment when I stepped foot on the boat; I wanted to believe that I would live a better life from then on. Since I'm asked these questions of late, I'm going to first talk about the events that I lived through and that traumatised my childhood, and then I'm going to continue with the rest …

Life at home

I remember, every Sunday mother would hurry us along to get ready for church. My parents' greatest care and worry was to do their duty to God, as advised by their parish priest. That's why they had nine children. Now, whether they had enough food to feed them, to clothe them or to send them to school, that wasn't their greatest concern. My father would always say: God will provide. The oldest boys started to voice their opinion on the matter. I remember one of them saying: Yes, father, God will provide, but the poor still have nothing. As for Kostakis, when they insisted he go to church, he would say, 'Oh, leave me alone. The same movie plays every time, with the same scenery!' And us scallywags would laugh behind our parents' backs and pretend to agree.

I didn't want to go to church because I didn't have decent clothes and my shoes were so worn. I was always worried in case the other wealthier girls in my class saw me and so I would squeeze myself in between the women parishioners as much as I could. I would feel myself growing smaller amongst them and they would look down on me as though my very presence sullied their image.

I would often admire them, timidly and secretly touching their dresses very gently so that they didn't notice. Caressing their dresses gave me such joy that, young child that I was, I imagined that the women that wore such beautiful dresses and shoes must be so happy. I imagined myself in their place so that I could feel the same joy. How innocent I was. My God, how pure is a child's mind! And yet, why do children have to suffer so much, why does their mind have to expand and be plagued by so many questions. As far as the church was concerned, my first and most pressing question came about when I was nine years old. And I will tell you about the incident that clouded my mind, made me feel dizzy until I thought clearly and logically about it, even though I was so young.

There was a poverty-stricken woman who lived near the sea, whose husband had died leaving her with five young boys. It was around four to five o'clock one afternoon, the time that the neighbourhood women would get together and chat – that was their only entertainment as no one had a television or radio as far as I knew. The women told jokes, a bit of gossip, and sometimes would even recount something risqué. We could tell when this was happening by the way they laughed, particularly if Vasilo or Alexandra was in their company.

We pretended to be indifferent but drew closer and closer because we wanted to learn their secrets. But heaven help us if they noticed us around! They would chase us off yelling, 'Get lost you ratbags! Aren't you ashamed of yourselves.' Now I don't think that we had anything to feel ashamed about. We just wanted to join in.

That afternoon though, instead of laughing at anything and everything, all you could discern was a look of grief on their faces.

We gathered a little further along from them, asking each other in turn, trying to work out what was wrong but no one was any the wiser. We looked around and noticed that Mimis was absent from our group of kids. And we all started desperately asking each other if anyone had seen him at school. Mimis, Panagiotaina's orphan child, was the cleverest of all of us and always knew how to entertain us with his stories every evening as we'd sit in the hollow stretch of ground that separated the houses from the train tracks. I started to go but Andreas, with eyes glistening, told us that Mimis was at school. Our faces shone with sheer joy. And just then, over towards the bridge, we saw Mimis running barefoot towards us. He seemed overcome, shocked, telling us that as he was passing Mrs Stavroula's house he saw that they had rested a casket against the wall like they do when someone has died and that it was Triantafyllos.

Straight away I remembered that last year it was Lefteris who had died. The poor woman was losing her sons one by one to tuberculosis. What could the wretched woman do? The sea battered against her door, one small room with no heating; there was no income either, apart from some money from the rich and the Good Samaritans. The Good Samaritans were a group of wealthy ladies that provided for the poor. They got together to pass the time as they were bored. They'd drink their coffee and would organise to give the odd penny to those in need. Anyway, it was better than nothing.

And so we learned about Triantafyllos' funeral and we agreed to all go to church. I found myself next to the coffin and my mind couldn't get around the fact that such a handsome young man could be lying in there, dead. His devastated mother long knew the fate that awaited her. Her doctor had told her straight out. Take your children and go, to a mountain, to a dry climate and look after yourselves. But this poor woman couldn't hope to find the money to do what the doctor ordered. That day in the church next to the dead Triantafyllo and seeing just the priest, his mother, the women of the neighbourhood and us scallywags, barefoot and in rags, something happened inside me and I protested. I started an internal dialogue with the women, the Good Samaritans, and with all the wealthy people in our town. Why don't you all give this family a good house far from the sea and why don't you make sure that they have enough food, clothes, medicine, why … a thousand 'whys' circled my mind and caused it to revolt that day against all those well-dressed men and women, against the priests and everyone who I knew was well-to-do!

But all my questions were of no help at all and the unfortunate Mrs Stavroula lost all her sons. The only son to escape this fate was Andreas. His nickname was Wicks (I remember he sold wicks, candles and icons outside of churches). He would often come to our humble home asking for some food. My mother knew his circumstances and would give him the little that we could spare but it was never enough – and yet, he survived. And when I returned to Greece years later I bumped into him on the road towards Kouloura. He didn't recognise me and begged me for some money. It plunged me into my memories; it broke my heart.

School years

Poverty is horrific. I remember feeling so ashamed in school of my clothes, my shoes, my books and my pencil which were not like those of the other children. This caused a lot of suffering for me just like it did for those children who shared my fate.

Oh how well I remember at recess a good-hearted girl whose mother always gave her something to eat. She often had baked quince and Sophia always shared some with me. She understood that I didn't have such luxuries as I never had any food with me.

How delicious that quince tasted! I've never eaten anything as tasty even though these days I can buy as much food as I like. Hunger, you see … I was always starving back then whereas now I never have a chance to feel hungry; I'm always eating something. In our times, other children elsewhere are hungry and are suffering, perhaps even more than we did. We see them on the television every day, thousands of them dying, helpless …

We could help those people and I know that many are being helped, just like others helped us back then, when we were so in need, through UNRRA. This shouldn't be overlooked. There is definitely kindness in the world and I'm going to write about it later.

A wealthy old woman called Moustina lived in our neighbourhood. Her son, whose wife had died leaving him with their little boy called Souli, had a food store. His brother had also died, his wife as well – everyone seemed to be dying back then – leaving their children, Alekos and Beba, orphaned.

The uncle looked after the children, three in all. He also had two maids, one to raise the children, while the other looked after his elderly mother, Moustina, and, most days, her granddaughter Beba stayed with them as well, as this kept her grandmother happy. Their house was the last one in our small town. It was a beautiful two-storey house with a tree-filled garden, with vegetables and flowers; to my child's eyes the house resembled a palace, the garden looked like a paradise. They had a dog, cats, birds, two or three ewes, a goat and if I remember correctly a little donkey. The house had one level with separate rooms: one was called the drawing-room and the other was a small room, a bedroom, where Beba used to sleep when she stayed with her grandmother. The other half of the house was a dining-room and kitchen that had a window that oversaw grandmother Moustina's bed. There was a storeroom on the ground floor; the other half was used to house the animals. I was friends with Beba and the grandmother liked me, just as she liked my mother who would often go in the evenings and give her cupping-glass therapy. They were the wealthy people of our neighbourhood and so when mother would return from old-Moustina's place, we knew that she would bring us something to eat, bread, fruit, and something from the garden. The grandmother would tell my mother that she could gather up anything that fell on the ground, 'go on, Eleni, go and gather some olives'. They were of no use to them but for us who were poverty-stricken, struggling to feed ten souls, they were salvation, they were life.

The grandmother would often ask me to help with the chores, things like bringing her wood and lighting the fire at dusk. Beba and I did many cheeky things! I remember that when the paper factory siren went off at ten each evening, we would scream and jump up and down deliberately creating commotion so that the grandmother didn't hear it and tell me to go home so they could go to sleep! Another time I remember that she had a huge cooked fish in the pantry-box for her evening meal. All afternoon Beba and I picked at it, a little bit here, a little there, until there was nothing left but the head and the skeleton covered by the skin. When the time came for the grandmother to have her evening meal – the poor thing couldn't see very well – she had trouble finding any flesh. 'You ratbags, what has happened to the fish?' 'Oh, the cat ate it', Beba replied and we laughed sneakily. She was a kind soul, she didn't tell us off much, often muttering under her breath, talking to herself, 'Oh those scallywags, they don't understand what they're doing, they're young, they don't need much to have a good time.' Perhaps she remembered a similar scene when she, herself, was a little girl.

Our household suffered so much during the war years, but grandmother Moustina was always kind. Whenever I went to her house she always gave me something to eat.

The coat

My mother had made me a coat out of a blanket that had been given to her by UNRRA. She dyed it a sort of garnet colour and had sewn two huge pockets on the inside, somewhere for me to put a few sultanas that she had advised me to put in my mouth when I was really hungry. The other kids in the neighbourhood and my brothers and sisters would call my pockets 'stealing bags'. And when I'd go to grandmother Moustina's house, my siblings would tell me to wear the coat with the concealed pockets. These pockets actually helped us to survive the war years. As wise men say, all is fair in times of war. They must have known what they were talking about. So, this is how it happened.Whenever grandmother Moustina sent me down to the basement to feed the animals with the barley meal that she had made into a type of porridge for them, I would fill my pockets to the brim. I was just a frightened child and I felt so guilty to be stealing from her. Now, looking back, I see that this was an act of mercy towards my brothers and sisters.

When I'd go back upstairs near the elderly woman again, I couldn't wait to get out of there because I knew how many mouths were waiting for this Manna from heaven. I'd get up and say I had to get going because it was dark. 'Oh Litsa, Litsa', the old lady would say, 'it's still early. Stay a little longer to keep me company.' I tried to be especially nice to her, would put her to bed, do any last-minute chores, and disappear! As soon as I opened the door to our house, everyone would call out with one voice, 'did you bring anything, did you?' The cooking would start straight away.

I would empty my pockets, mother would make a lovely batter and make us pancakes. My father would make the sign of the cross and thank God in gratitude. Tomorrow God would provide again. As for me, I knew that if I didn't go to old Moustina's place to gather some olives from the ground to get made into a little oil to eat with the wild grass that my mother gathered, then we would eat plain boiled wild grass. Unfortunately, God didn't provide for the poor, just the wealthy.

Tragic events

From a very young age I started to question and doubt those who were supposedly believers and good Christians. I am one of those children who lived through the war in all its tragedy. Horror, starvation, indescribable feelings that can only be understood by those who lived through them as well. How could I ever forget the day that I found myself in the Town Square? I witnessed something that I can never forget.

Our square had trees right around. On each of those trees, the Germans had hanged a fine young man. The Germans were standing on the hotel's balcony, rifles in hand, finger on the trigger, ready to fire. They had given orders that no one was to come near otherwise they would be killed on the spot. There were mothers wailing and children like me standing there without being able to do anything to alleviate their pain. Who can help these souls at times like that? Absolutely no one, except for Mother Nature who somehow gives us boundless courage.

I remember another event that I live through again and again. I had gone to Themistokli's bakery to buy a little bread. Just as I was leaving with the loaf under my arm the sirens started blaring demonically. We had to duck to the nearest shelter. I pushed my way into one and it was packed with so many people. We were there for hours listening to the bombing and wondering if this was the end.

The times in those shelters were difficult, unbearable. You felt like dying because the hours were endless and when someone needed to relieve themselves they would go to the far corner but the stench was disgusting. When the final siren sounded, signalling that the danger had passed and we could go home, we were just wrecked. The faces that emerged filled you with pity. Your soul felt wounded at the piteous state of humanity.

The old man

With such a feeling of terror in my heart, I made my way home. I was just a young child. It took me about half an hour to reach our house and little did I know that I would face even more tragic events as they unfolded down the track. As soon as I walked into our humble little house I saw someone there I didn't know – an old man that my mother started to say was my uncle and so on. I remember he was holding a heshian bag filled with bread and cheese. When we'd eaten a little portion of frumenty that passed for a meal we went to sleep.

Our visitor decided to honour our hospitality by giving us a tiny slice of bread each. We had seen his bag and hungered after its contents but he hung it up on the wall, over his bed, to watch over its contents. But hunger is a strong motivator and makes inroads. My two oldest brothers must have kept watch till the old man went to sleep, then took a portion each to calm their hunger. This is what must have happened as, the next morning, the old man could be heard complaining to my mother that the children ate the bread that he had organised to last him till he returned home.

Even at such a young age I recall that it made such a bad impression on me that he could complain about hungry children taking a little bit of his bread. I hated injustice from my childhood years. When my mother had finished scolding the older boys for their bad deed, we all ran outside to play and to criticise our old relative who, in our minds, should have shared his bread with us. After a while mother called us back inside as she wanted to tell us something. Mother, father and the old man had discussed something and agreed upon it. They simply wanted to inform us about their decision.

And so, they told us that they had organised for the old man to take us home with him. We would work for him in exchange for a plate of food so we wouldn't die. Thanos would help out the old man's son in the fields, whereas they wanted me to help his wife with the household chores, to tend to and feed the animals, and to help out in the fields. Our parents told us that we were lucky children that our uncle came to save us from dying. However, even though I was just a child, I didn't see it as logical at all. The time came to say goodbye to our parents and siblings, the old man took us and we boarded the train for an unknown fate. My every instinct told me, warned me, that this life would not be at all good. I would be living far from my parents, my brothers and sisters, and my friends.

As in a dream I recall the train stopping somewhere, the old man pushing us out as though we were sheep to the slaughter. There we met some other strange people with two horses. They plonked us on the saddle, me and my brother together on one, the old man on the other, and we started out for the unknown. It was the first time I had ever climbed on to a horse and I was trembling with fear, terrified I would fall to the ground and die. My little heart was fluttering from worry and pain.

When it started to grow dark, the tears started rolling down my face and I wanted nothing more than to be back in my humble house, playing with the neighbourhood children, even if I was barefoot and hungry.

When we'd been travelling with the horses for about four hours we finally came to a stop and were told that we had reached home. The village was called Arfara. The old lady, with lamp in hand, came out with her son to greet us. When they took me down from the horse I was so stiff that I couldn't move. My brother, who was five years older, started to push me whispering that I shouldn't act like an idiot. He couldn't possibly understand that, at that moment, I truly was an idiot. People pushed me around whenever they wanted to. Even though it was late, the old lady smiled and was kind to us, beckoning us to come inside and eat something, as we must be hungry after such a long journey.

We sat at the table near the corner that was covered in plentiful food.

If that lovely spread was in my own poor house I'd be so happy and I say this because those of us who lived in towns had a much harder time of it than those who lived in the villages. For us poverty-stricken families, the father managing to buy a loaf of bread and bringing it home to feed ten children, was an impressive achievement. This was the fate of the poor. As for the rich, they always somehow managed to always do well and to enjoy every kind of delicacy.

The experience that deeply wounded me as a child was every time my mother would cut my playing short only to wash my feet near the well and send me to Sotiropoulos or to one of the Good Samaritan ladies to give me some money to buy a morsel of bread or half a bag of beans.

Oh, how traumatised I felt upon reaching their door and ringing the bell, waiting for the maid to open and me, crestfallen, trembling, looking to the ground in shame, hearing my voice – that sounded alien to me in those moments – uttering that my mother had sent me to ask for some assistance to get through the day. The maid would immediately run to the drawing-room upstairs, you see the houses of the rich were always large with beautiful gardens full of flowers. and inform the lady of the house about this and that. Until the maid returned, I had dreamed a thousand dreams and countless disappointing scenarios constricted my poor little heart.

I knew that if I got a handout how happy the faces around me would be that evening, all huddled together, after we'd eaten something ... I also knew the disappointment and devastation when the lady of the house would appear at the stairs to tell me, in an absolutely apathetic and cold tone, that the Good Samaritans hadn't organised anything yet and to come back next week. At that moment I became a nothing from the shame and disappointment and wanted to die, because I knew that as long as I was alive, mother would send me there again the following week. No, I couldn't stand this Golgotha; it had become the nightmare of my childhood.

All of these things passed through my mind like a movie that first night at this strange house, high on a mountain, where I was to work and be provided with food and so survive. That's why my parents sent me here:

to survive. When I'd eaten something, the old lady, seeing that I was dizzy from exhaustion and lack of sleep, beckoned me to where she had fixed a place for me to sleep, and that in the morning she would tell me about my chores. She took me to the room that they had as a sort of formal room and put a quilt on the floor as a mattress. I remember that this made an impression on me and I immediately formed the opinion that this old lady had a kind soul.

When I was left alone in the dark, instead of drifting off to sleep given how exhausted I was, I stayed awake trying to make sense of the events of the last few days that led to my finding myself in a strange house so far from my home; far away from all my friends. Playing with them every afternoon, gathering wild grasses, fallen fruit or olives that had fallen to the ground, and often going to the beach to gather wood or debris that the sea had washed up, made our lives happy, even if some of these games were dangerous in our quest to find something to help us survive one more day. Because heaven help us if the rural policeman caught us in the act of taking something that, in his opinion, was stealing. We would go through hell begging him to let us off the hook. He would then take all that we had gathered in our baskets and would do us the favour of letting us go home, threatening us with the warning that if he ever caught us in someone else's garden again he would dig our grave in it …

And all of us kids of the war and of hunger would return to our homes disappointed and with empty baskets but always in the company of Mimis, the orphan, the incredibly smart child of the group who always knew how to make up some story that would drag us out of our misery and into far-away worlds where children lived carefree lives, reminding us that tomorrow the siren might signal the end of the war. And so, as I was thinking about Mimis' fairytale about the end of the war, sleep overtook me and gave me wings to be with my friends once again.

The dream

It was around dusk and we were playing hide and seek. I had hidden behind Fidia's fence and near me was a blackberry bush that I absentmindedly ate a few unripened berries from. They didn't have a chance to ripen as we'd eat them and then get stomach aches.

I felt the need to wee in my hiding place and I enjoyed that as well. Just as I was enjoying my friends and my hiding place and everything, I woke up from the sounds of sheep, donkeys, clucking of chickens, all this music coming from the basement where all the animals were housed.

When I opened my eyes and realised where I was, I lost myself, felt so enbittered and didn't want to live. As soon as I came to, I sensed a wetness on the lower part of my body. I knew that I had not weed hiding behind Fidia's fence but on the quilt of the kindly old lady in the new home that I found myself in. I felt like fainting, I didn't know what to do but, luckily, no one was home. I got up and hesitantly walked from room to room. No one was there – they had all gone to the fields. So I had time to think about how I would sort out the mess I made during the night.

I folded the quilt and put it in the blanket pile where the other sheets and blankets were kept, one on top of the other. I ran to the kitchen, grabbed a bucket of water, and started wetting the floor from the front door to the place where I was sleeping, and where the floorboards had expanded. I looked at it all, looked at it again and my plan sort of satisfied me and I calmed down.

Just before midday my aunty returned and, once she had tended to the animals in the basement, she came upstairs and asked, smiling, if I'd had a good night's sleep and what all the water was that was spilled here and there. I started telling her a made-up story about a chicken that came inside and filled the house with droppings, especially in the area where I slept and that I mopped it all up. The kind old lady, ever-smiling, understood exactly what had happened and told me not to worry that I wet the bed and that it only happened because I was frightened and that I would soon get used to it here. She did say only that I shouldn't have put the soiled quilt in the bedding pile because everything would become smelly and mouldy. She went and got everything and put them out to dry.

That's how our life started there on the high mountain, in the village that they called Arfara. A difficult, harsh life for an eight-year-old child who had to work hard as though she were an 18-year-old young adult. Now, when I remember these days every night before going to sleep, I say this and I believe it: parents should never send their children away because these children suffer, they are wounded and these wounds never heal throughout their life.

Life on the mountain

One day followed the next with hard work and worry. From the crack of dawn till nightfall the hours somehow passed. The work was arduous and heavy for a little girl of eight. But when twilight started to descend, my heart ached and I wanted nothing more than to be back in my humble home again, in my old neighbourhood with my friends. And one thought always took precedence in my child's mind. Because I knew that our house in Aigion was next to a train line, I tried to work out how I would reach Akrata and from there walk until I finally reached our house. That was the dream; daily life continued and got worse. My brother was usually with Thimio, the old man's son. They went to the fields with the cattle and did numerous farm jobs. My aunty and I did the housework, fed the chickens, the goats, would go and gather the lentils, walnuts, almonds, oats for the animals and lots more besides.

The journeys we took, as we followed the animals, were treacherous. We had to be very careful at each and every step as one stumble would mean falling off the cliff to our death. The land was very wild; the pathways we had to pass through to reach each destination were very dangerous.

But what left its mark on my life from those days and which has haunted me for the rest of my life, didn't happen on the dangerous pathways that I trembled in fear while crossing, but down on some other land that they owned in the valley, at a location called Mavrendi. It was there that they had a small house divided into two rooms, one where people stayed when they were working at the pruning, digging, harvesting and any other jobs that needed doing each season. The other room was where they put the animals.

The room where we stayed had two beds on wooden posts stuck directly into the soil. In the middle was a fireplace that was on all night during the winter, its flames keeping us company as did the crackling of the logs. There was a table, two chairs and a cupboard in the corner where they put foodstuffs. It was in that room that I and the old man stayed when we had work to do in the fields.

One night when we returned from the field, we fed the aminals, lit the fire, had a bite to eat and while I set about clearing the table, the old man called me over to rub his back. He had taken off his clothes from the waist up and was warming himself in front of the fire. As I approached him, half-naked as he was, with white hair on his chest, an image immediately flaired up before me and I didn't see the old man anymore but an animal from the neighbouring room, but to be honest I couldn't make out what animal that was, a goat, a cow, a mule, maybe even an animal I was unfamiliar with. That night my nightmare began.

When I had rubbed his back as he instructed me to, I moved away to sit on the little stool. I had an instictive fear about what was going to happen next. He got up, red all over, and started making licentious gestures towards me. I was shaken, sprang up and started getting away from him, seeking some possible refuge in that wilderness where there wasn't a soul in sight. As I was being chased around the room, a terrified little girl of eight, I jumped on to the bed imagining that it would provide some way of escape. The old man stretched out his arm and with a satisfied smile said, 'You can't escape me now. Come and lie with me because I'm cold.'

I was trembling like a little bird the first time they put it in a cage. I was crouching, became smaller. I felt like this tiny little thing that wanted nothing more than to develop wings and to fly to my home and, even if I died of hunger, so be it. For a young child, what I was living through was worse than dying. The dirty old man continued with the lurid gestures. He wanted to have sex but thank heavens, at this age, it was impossible and so he tried in the most immoral way to satisfy his urges. And, of course, he knew that what he was doing was bad and he started to whisper to me that if I ever dared to tell my aunt he would kill me with the axe.

I ran out crying to the next room where the animals were and sat on the ground so that he wouldn't find me, but as he came through the door to catch me the animals moved and he could work out where I was. And then he said, 'Come quickly inside and I won't touch you.' I was living through this horror, begging for the dawn to break, to see the light of day and then would feel a little better. When I'd go into the room again I was beset by my childish fantasies; that I would open the door and flee. Where would I go though? Outside there was dense forest, there were no people anywhere and I was terrified of the forest.

I remember that they often loaded the horse with produce for me to take to Arfara and most of the roads that I had to traverse were through dense forest and my little heart would pound from fright and my right hand, when I'd reach my destination, was heavy and stiff from constantly making the sign of the cross. But I didn't do my cross in a natural way, as I was scared that if I extended my arm some wild animal would pounce and tear it off. As I said, I was just a small child.

This time in my life left a deep wound. From then, every evening when it would start to grow dark, I would be overcome by such a feeling of terror that I would start to cry. When we finished all the work and it was time to leave Mavrendi, as we'd turn into Arfara, I felt a little relieved and even sort of happy. But the old man understood how I felt and the minute we neared the house and walked through the gate he would remind me as to what would befall me if I ever told his wife.

The old woman would come out with the lamp to greet us and Thanos and Thimios would take over the unloading of the animals, they would feed them and then we would all get together to eat. And later on, around the hearth, eating walnuts and sultanas and roasting chestnuts, I would try to distract myself so that I wouldn't remember any of the scenes that I lived through, but every time that a chestnut would pop or a log would crackle, I was immediately back in that far away house with my executioner. Seeing him now smiling opposite me I felt disgust and would ask myself how he could just sit there chatting and smiling, and how was it that everyone in the village respected him as the finest gentleman, greeting him and taking their hat off to him when he'd pass by?

In the square there was a huge plane tree and two cafes. The men would gather there every evening and whenever the village dance took place, all the officials and all the villagers would assemble there. One day when we were all there this idea came into my head: to jump on to one of the small round tables that they usually have in cafes and yell out informing them as to who exactly that man is that everyone respects. To then finally get some relief, organising that they send me home immediately. I was just a child, you see, with a child's mind. How I longed for my home every evening. It was a torment for me. I was lost in my thoughts and hope. I was hoping for the war to end so that they could take us home. I didn't like anything at all about this place; a wild and desolate landscape full of worry. Whenever I had to take the goats to pasture and one would stray I would run to reach it but the ground was so uneven that if I ever I were to stumble I would end up in the ravine below. Mind you, I often hoped that I would slip and fall and so leave this life.

Around the hearth the old man would often announce to his wife that we had to go to Mavrendi because there were chores that needed tending to, that the resin would be dripping from the trees. Those two years in this hellish place left me with not one good memory, apart from the smell of the resin and the pine trees in the forest, a layer of solace for my child's tormented body. Whenever I heard the conversations about Mavrendi I knew what was waiting for me and yet I didn't have the strength to react. Those two years that I spent away from my family had a terrible effect on me that lasted for the rest of my life.

When the war ended and the Germans left, the old lady could see that I was suffering, that I couldntn't get used to the life there, sobbing uncontrolably every evening at nightfall, wailing that I wanted to go home. When my mother came to pick us up, she was so disappointed to see us looking like wild animals. Her first words that I heard were, 'What happened to you, my children, and you've become so wild?' Thanos, with his dark, thick curly hair untamed on his young years, plentiful food, clean air, and who knows what they got up to with Thimios.

I remember once when we were harvesting a field and they had taken me along to give them a hand. In the afternoon, they lumbered me with the animal and sent me to Arfara. I travelled on foot as the animal was loaded with produce. I don't know the exact distance but that journey seemed endless to me. Utterly exhausted and suffering I finally reached the house. The old lady was perplexed and started to tell me off, saying that I shouldn't have left because she knew why those cheeky boys had sent me away; they wanted to sleep with some shameless girl.

The truth is that during the occupation everyone did whatever they needed to do to survive. I remember that many young boys and girls from the neighbouring towns would come to the village and, as the villagers harvested and gathered their stacks, they would gather any remaining bits that hadn't been noticed by the owners. That particular afternoon I remember the group was made up of three girls and two boys. It seems that Thimios, like the wealthy boy that he was, had organised with a girl to spend the night together with the promise of a little wheat in exhange.

Things like that happened back then.

Return home – the 'boutsi'

As I was saying, when the Germans left, mother came to take us home. She got a fright when she saw us. We were two wild animals. With the fresh air and plentiful food, Thanos had grown large and was really like a wild ram. Me, on the other hand, in my rags and wearing old soldiers' boots, with my wild-sounding voice that I think was from the water, and from the life I experienced there, I was like a wild little goat.

My poor mother didn't recognise her own children! She drew me close to her, hugged me and told me she was taking us home so that life could go on like before. She quietly assured me that once home, we would slowly calm down, this was just a storm that will pass. I got a new nickname back at home, boutsi, and I'll tell you how.

My oldest sister had been adopted by her Godmother and lived in the town five minutes from the bus stop. My mother thought that it made sense to go there first so that we could all see each other. As I said, I was wearing an old cotton dress with a check pattern and old boots and my voice had become wild and rough. I had a hessian bag where they had put my 'payment' for all my work: some pieces of leather, and on my belt the old lady had hung a little purse with some coins in it. She was a kind and compassionate woman. When I left, she kissed me, hugged me and wished me good luck. When my sister and I had kissed each other, everyone started asking me what was in my bag. With my rough voice I started saying that they gave me some leather to make shoes because they killed some cows, horses and goats. I also proudly announced, in a loud voice, that I have a boutsi. I didn't call it a 'purse' because, for some reason, boutsi was how it sounded to me when I first heard this word. Who knows what image I presented at that moment. Sophia broke down into hysterical laughter, clutching at her stomach.

From that day, whenever we would all get together everyone would beg me to recount, exactly as I had done on my first day back, what I had in my bag when I returned from Arfara. And so I became the entertainment and my audience fell about laughing. We didn't have a television in those days and we would amuse ourselves with things like that. When we came back home, Thimios and I were the main topic of conversation. It seems that for the neighbourhood and for our friends we were very strange creatures and they approached us as though we had arrived from another planet. How could we have changed so much in two years? And yet we had. The person who said that 'whichever teacher you are exposed to will determine what lessons you will learn', either had personal experience that gave rise to this proverb, or they were very wise. Whether you want to learn these lessons or not, life will throw them at you.

It was the mountain, the clean air, the water, the wild landscape and we gave ourselves over to this environment in adolescence and the environment moulded us according to the material at its disposal. But we didn't give of ourselves entirely. We always fixed out gaze on our small town that glowed against the stars like a planet every night. I could never come to terms with life on the land. I think of those people, I empathise with them, I pity them. They work hard, very hard; their loneliness terrifies me. I like living amongst people, in commotion. I like listening to many conversations, going to the theatre, taking in an art exhibition. You have so many things to observe whereas in a remote village life is restricted. Of course I say this now, but even back then I did not like village life.

And so here I am, at my destination, in my humble little house and with my young friends.

Our house

Even though the war had ended, our poverty didn't end with it. We were a large family with no income. We had our little house which always remained unfinished. They had built the frame high, for two storeys, but had never managed to actually build the second floor. I remember the beams that bags of pasta and frumenty and other foodstuffs hung from to sustain us during the winter. One room was the so-called drawing-room. There was a double bed there that my parents slept in, a cupboard that was virtually empty, a vanity mirror, a velvet sofa which was completely frayed for as long as I could recall, a type of chest of drawers, a beautiful piece of furniture, with drawers either side and two little doors in the middle with engravings, while the top was made out of marble.

That's where mother placed whatever sweets she had, Turkish delight or traditional orange syrup spoon sweets, so that she might have something to offer a visitor to our home. Not that we ever had many guests but mother was a good homemaker and took care of everything. There was a towel rack with 'good morning' engraved on it from which hung a solitary towel used by ten people. In the corner, as we entered the room, we stored our folded blankets and rugs one on top of the other and every night we would place them on the floor and all sleep next to each other.

The two oldest boys slept in the other room that we used as a kitchen and dining room. One bed was near the table and so we used it as seating. There was a narrow cupboard where mother housed all her worldly belongings, something that my older brothers always teased her about. There were a few glasses, some coffee cups, a box of sugar, another with coffee, and a vase that she stored the tea in, not mountain tea but another type called European tea, I have no idea why. On the bottom she had the oil, vinegar and salt. Next to this cupboard was the so-called plate stand, underneath which was a wooden chest that we had lined with paper and newspapers, while next to this casing in the corner was an outline of a window that was never fully built.

That's where they put the wash basin, put some makeshift concrete on the bottom part of the window, opened a round hole that led outside and every morning we would all wash there. That's where we washed our dishes when it was very cold or raining. If the weather was fine, we would go to the well which was more pleasant. Whenever I washed the dishes I would become deeply upset as this hand basin was truly terrible; it always had an oily residue around it and stunk of mould. Further along from the basin was the fireplace and next to this in the corner was a rickety old moth-eaten table, above which hung a small cage where people placed items of food. For, you see, in those times we didn't have refrigerators although the cage lay empty as we had nothing to put in it. I remember that this cage always caused friction in our household because if there was ever any leftover food mother would place it in there for later in the evening. But she never found anything later on. How could anything remain with so many growing children? But there were always interrogations to try to get to the truth of who ate it. Looking back now, I often wonder how we survived and didn't die from starvation and poverty.

I remember in the afternoons when we'd play with the other children and forget our hunger and wretchedness, mother would call out to us to go and gather some log to light the fire. Where that log was meant to come from I'll never know. We had raided fences, fields full of thorns, we had even walked over an hour away to a village with a river and gather anything that flowed down from the mountain. That walk was lovely because there was an orchard with apple trees. Most of our group kept guard outside, while two of us girls would enter, filling our skirts with apples. All along the journey we had a great time eating the apples and felt happier about carting the wood. Poverty, poverty, poverty, hunger but courage as well!

I remember she would often send us to gather some husks from Fidia's field so that we could have some light in the evening while we ate. One child and then the other would take it in turns, trying to fan the flame, throwing in a handful of husks every now and then to keep a little light in the room as we ate some frumenty or vegetable. Us tormented children of the Occupation went through so much. Our minds worked overtime and we grew up before our time.

Panagiotoula Giatena, the pious one

As I have written earlier, our oldest sister, Sofia, had been adopted by her Godmother whose name was Panagiotoula Giatena. They had quite a bit of money; they lacked nothing and she was quite religious. Their two-storey house was behind their local church. Given that she didn't have to travel far, just cross a road, she was never absent from church and she had never held any other book in her hands apart from the New Testament.

I can see her now, right in front of me in her seat, as she had a permanent pew. Her hair was white, she was thin, by all accounts a distinguished looking woman, even beautiful, perhaps even very beautiful. But I didn't like her. She seemed very cold. I also see her in the afternoons sitting in a little bedroom surrounded by walls filled with icons, looking out of her half-shuttered window. She, herself, could see all of the movement outside, while no one could see that someone was sitting behind the shutters.

I had never seen her carry out any work, nothing, no work of any description, except for reading and taking in the New Testament. Light duties were carried out by our Sophia and the heavier jobs were undertaken by Anna, the young maid.

I really liked going there even though after the long walk, upon ringing the bell, Giatena would often not allow anyone to open the door to me, while I was certain that she was there in her seat behind the shutters. And now that I am a grown up I think back to this. Since I knew that she didn't want to be disturbed, why did I keep going? Well, I had my reasons. As I mentioned before, they were wealthy and I really liked being in that environment and I wanted nothing more than for us to have a civilised house like that. Here and there, Sophia would give me a handful of sultanas or a lolly and that made me completely happy.

In the summers there, we would sit in the back garden of the house. They had a wooden seat of the kind you see in parks and that are called benches, a large mandarin tree and lots of flowers. The view was exceptional. The eye could relax in this breathtaking landscape; far into the horizon you could see the fishing-boats like white dots moving on the sea.

Outside there, we would contrive anything we could to pass the time happily. And the last scene was always the one that I would present. They would make me play out the scene when I returned from Arfara. When I was about to say that I had brought back some cow, some horse and some goat hides, Sophia and Anna would burst out laughing, we would all forget ourselves, enjoying the moment. But as soon as Giatena heard the cackling she would come out and remind me that I had to get on home before it got dark.

How I longed for her to forget so that they might have to keep me there for the night. But no matter how much I prayed each night for this to happen, it never did. I was, you see, just an innocent young child and I believed in what my parents told me. However, I slowly began to understand for myself what I should believe in. Many who followed the ways of the Lord were the most evil people I knew and their deeds taught me well.

Against all odds, with half a pencil and tattered shoes, I finished primary school. There was no way for me to continue. I had to learn some sort of trade.

At the dressmaker's

My Godmother was a dressmaker and it was arranged for me to go and learn dressmaking from her. Our house was on the outskirts of Aigion near the sea and it took me about an hour, walking briskly, to get there, morning and night, and at midday. In Greece, everything stops at midday, when people eat and lie down for two hours. So my mother reasoned that it would be easier for me to go to Giatena's house at lunchtime, to pass the time and to eat whatever mother had packed for me, usually bread and cheese and, here and there, an egg. So that was settled, and life continued with my soul in a state of exasperation at all that I saw around me and all that I experienced.

Sophia's Godmother was respected by Aigion society as being an esteemed person because, as just about all of you know, when someone is well-to-do and is God-fearing, that person is considered a somebody. But even though I was just a little girl I would look at all this, my young mind trying to make sense of it all, failing to reconcile all that I observed and really suffering in the process. I'll now give you an example that perplexed me and made me wonder what sort of Christian woman my sister Sophia's Godmother actually was.

As arranged, I would go to their house at lunchtime to save me the hour's walk home, to avoid the heat and fatigue, have a bite to eat, to pass the time till I went back to my Godmother's house. At that time the ritual was that Giatena, Sophia and Anna, the maid, the three of them would gather around the table, a prayer would be said with lowered heads and hands crossed in front of them, and they would start eating. I would hear and see all this through a crack in the kitchen door, because that's where I was allowed to sit, just a poor child eating my meagre bread, being made to feel that I was lucky to be allowed inside such an impressive house.

I was really disturbed by all of this and, even though so young, my mind revolted against the injustice and I couldn't understand what sort of Christian woman she was. I would imagine myself seated among them, eating their delicious food with them, and I lived with the secret hope that she would realise that it wasn't fair that I, a poverty-stricken child, should eat all alone in the kitchen and that the next day she would invite me to sit with them as well. But in the three years that I continued to go to this house, this honour was never bestowed upon me.

My Godmother, Nikoleta, the dressmaker

I was twelve years old when I went to my Godmother's to learn dressmaking. I was too young to imagine what I would encounter there.

My Godmother had a husband that she kept as a formality, I will explain this further down, and two children, Laki who had completed high school and a daughter, Maroula who was about twelve-thirteen years old. They didn't own a house, living in a rented home. This home had steep stairs with no railing and an empty space beneath them that terrified me. Those stairs were the bane of my childhood. I don't know why they frightened me so much but I was impelled to go up and down these stairs countless times a day.

Back then in Greece, during those years just after the world war and the civil war, if you went off to become a dressmaker, you needed to accept that first you had to become a servant. And in the afternoon, if you had a little free time, you could sit in the sewing room with five or six other girls, that had also passed through the servant stage, hoping to learn within this atmosphere the art of dressmaking.

You had to sweep in the mornings, airing the rugs on the balcony that were full of cotton threads that never came unstuck no matter how forcefully you shook them. You then had to take them off one by one because if any were still left on the rug my Godmother would send you to do the job again. You had to take a cup of milk to Laki in bed, wake him up, and fend off his advances as he tried to grab your hand and so on. I think that at some stage my Godmother cottoned on to what was happening, advising her son that it was a sin to flirt with me because, according to our religion, I was his spiritual sister.

Thereafter, my Godmother would send Antigone to wake him up because she was a beautiful blond girl of about eighteen or nineteen that she liked and wanted as a daughter-in-law, and that Laki also liked and so they tried to make this happen. But there was no way that Antigone would take Laki as her husband whose father was drunk every night. The girl was worried that the son would follow in his father's footsteps. But thirty years later I returned to Greece for a holiday and went to see them all. Laki was married to a beautiful and kind woman, one of his daughters had married while the other daughter was highly educated and with a very good position. He himself ran a jeweller's shop in the town centre of Aigio. Antigone never married, remaining with her ideas for company.

As for my Godfather, he lived in another world. He was a jeweller and, although he worked for someone else, in the town he was considered an excellent craftsman. He must have been, otherwise how was he kept on and paid given that he was almost always drunk. People would say that before going to the shop he would pass by the tavern for the glass of alcohol that was like a tonic that would fire him up, as he would say. Now, how he could manage those tiny instruments used to make jewellery and watches, I have no idea. That remained, for me, an eternal enigma.

I remember once when we were working through the night finishing off dresses in time for Easter that was approaching, my Godmother started to worry because my Godfather was very late in coming home. Had he fallen anywhere? And just then we heard the door creak and in he came swaying to and fro, with heavy footsteps, stumbling and the wall of the entrance shaking, and my poor Godfather, blind drunk, muttering: 'Katina, my child, move out of the way so I can pass.' His daughter, Maroula, who was with us at the time, gave her mother a despairing look.

I remember my Godmother becoming hysterical. She grabbed a pair of scissors, screaming that she would stab herself in the heart to be rid of this life. Anyway, my Godfather stumbled towards a dark bedroom. There was a small divan in there where the poor man slept, sobering up only to start the cycle all over again. I remember my late father saying that the route my Godfather always took was from Bastouna's to Zaira's. These were basement taverns and the puzzle is how all these men were able to go up and down the stairs while drunk? Somehow they managed it just fine and when you'd ever bump into them, you'd see them emerge with glowing eyes and a faint smile, blissfully happy.

My Godfather had died by the time I returned. He couldn't last any longer; the drink defeated him.

Soula and my Godmother

The truth is that I have very bad memories from those days spent with them. I will never forget the days when we had to do the washing. Soula was the real maid, let's say, and my job was to help her. She was a big girl, beautiful with brown hair, hailing from a village. Her mother had died and her father had remarried. He had brought Soula to my Godmother to learn dressmaking with the understanding that she would help out around the house, and would eat and sleep there. Poor, unfortunate girl, what you went through!

I remember that to wash the clothes we would go down to the back part of the house, we would light a fire and then go and cart buckets of water from the tap on the road. As far as I was concerned, I could bear anything. The only thing that would bring me to the brink of despair was when the time came to wash my Godfather's handkerchiefs and socks, as well as other soiled clothes of his that I really try not to remember. Horrific moments. I know I shouldn't really write these things down but I'm going to anyway. Maybe this will help me throw off the repulsion that this job left me with. And yet I think perhaps I'll leave it there: your imagination can no doubt conjure up what we went through.

When we didn't manage to make those filthy clothes, with caked on blood, snot and so on, as white as snow, my Godmother would make us wash them again. But not before she had yelled at us for being hopeless, lazy, filthy and other horrible things that was the norm back then when telling off children, treating us with such ridiculous strictness, abusing us and belting us over nothing. I'm not blaming anyone, everyone was undergoing their own tribulations; I don't even blame my Godmother.

Her husband was my Godfather and so she had no help or support. Perhaps the fact that she had to strive to make a living herself, trying to provide a future for her children, had toughened her mentally to the point where she was unaware of how she was treating us. In any case, for Soula and me the situation was unbearable and our only hope was for something to happen so that we could escape this environment.

I remember that in the afternoons I would feel terribly hungry and, when my Godmother was busy fitting a client, I would secretly go to a drawer where they kept the bread and eat a few bites, just a few so that no one would notice, my heart pounding to breaking point. I had been taught to perceive this as stealing and sinful.

The cherries

I am going to tell you about something funny that happened. My Godmother was originally from Kouloura, a little out of Aigion. Her brother and two sisters, both unmarried, lived in the ancestral home there. They owned a few small plots of land, some fruit trees and would often bring some of their produce to my Godmother.

One time they brought her a basket full of cherries, large delicious cherries, that were crisp and firm as a stone, which is how they got their name, stone-cherries. When us girls saw them our eyes bulged wide and they whet our appetite. Each of us started planning how we'd manage it, and when would be the best moment, to grab a few of those cherries. We started toing and froing, each girl secretly from the other, with the basket getting lighter. When she finished with her fittings, my Godmother made the sign of the cross, and rid herself of the evil eye because she was always plagued by the evil eye. I have to mention here that my Godmother was a beautiful woman, well-proportioned in height and weight, with curly hair that was very in fashion back then, cut short and dyed, she had lovely eyes and a sweet smile, she liked music and laughter, she was always well-dressed and, recognised as she was in Aigion as a talented dressmaker, she had made a name for herself. She, herself, believed that she was beautiful and exceptional and that, understandably, everyone must be jealous of her and always giving her the evil eye.

And so it was on this day as well. She told us that some woman gave her the evil eye and, after she had performed the ritual to get rid of it, asked Meropi, who was her favourite, to go and get a few cherries and wash them, so that, 'I can put some in my mouth to sweeten it as I have drunk enough poison today from their demands in the fittings'. Meropi, proud that she had become my Godmother's right hand person, got up all airs and graces, her stomach full and from a wealthy family, incapable of understanding the rest of us who had never known a full stomach. At that moment we were overcome by foreboding, because the time had come for us to pay for our wrongdoing in eating the cherries.

We could hear her footsteps heading towards the room where the basket with the cherries was and, a second later, we saw her standing at the door, showing the nearly empty basket to my Godmother. Oh! At that moment my Godmother started screaming abuse at us, calling us spoilt, thieves, ungrateful! That she was trying to enlighten us, to teach us the technique of dressmaking, that we are animals and that we should confess our sins during these holy days with Easter approaching.

Our neighbours, the Armenians

Our neighbourhood was beautiful, near the sea, a little far from the city centre. Aigion is a lovely small town. As is the case with many towns in Greece, there was the upper town and the lower town. The higher settlement and the lower one. In these settlements lived, and continue to live, many refugee families that came as a result of the Asia Minor Disaster. They were referred to as the refugee precincts. Lovely settlements with small houses, flowering gardens and beautiful-looking boys and girls. We lived in the area known as the Line, near the train station, also referred to as the Armenian precinct. Many poor families lived there, as well as Armenians, who had also been chased out of their homeland by the Turks, ending up as refugees. As was the case with the Greek refugees, the Armenians also had beautiful, small houses, well-looked after and clean, with beautiful gardens and beautiful children. The Armenians were good householders, they were hardworking, just like the immigrants here in Australia, serious-minded and family-oriented.

At the back of their houses they cultivated gardens with vegetables that each household needed. The men worked in the paper mills that, in those years, were a Manna from heaven. For those working there, it meant an end to their financial problems; they enjoyed a comfortable family life and lived well. The government supported the Armenians because they had no assets. It gave them work in the paper mills. This caused jealousy amongst the locals who felt that foreigners had come and taken all their jobs.

This, of course, didn't stop the children, the women and even the men from being friendly with them, passing their days in peaceful brotherhood. Jealousy did lie in wait, however, and sometimes broke out in arguments with nasty verbal abuse.

As I've mentioned many times, there was much poverty in our neighbourhood and it was natural to be jealous of those who somehow survived better than others. I remember the Armenians with love, I see them returning from the market with bags full of good things. It was unsurprising that those who didn't have a dime were envious that they couldn't also go and buy something. Us children grew up all together, we went to school together, learnt a trade together. I went with Mrs Maria's daughter Mahi, Athina went with Mrs Zois' son Vanes to become tailors. Christo was inseparable from Manoli. We loved each other, were inseparable and even now they are always in my thoughts keeping me company. I am full of scenes from that time, memories of joy and sorrow. I remember Mrs Martha, Mihalis' mother, who kept food for her husband, Agopian, a tall, well-built man like a giant. Agopian worked the afternoon shift at the factory and the poor man was always hungry. How could spinach and rice dishes and the like satisfy the hunger of such a big man? Until Agopian came home, the children ate whatever they could find. This is why Mrs Martha would hide his plate of food as best she could in the safest place possible so that the children wouldn't find it. If they found it, they would devour it, and in the evening she would have nothing to offer her husband. In those years we didn't have an abundance of food, like we do today, with our refrigerators and pantries. One afternoon, when us children had gone to their house and were playing hide and seek, Mrs Martha was working on something in the kitchen. I don't know why, but I decided to hide under one of the beds.

And what should I see, but a huge earthen bowl, covered with a lid? I uncovered it and saw that it was full of food. I cannot tell you how delighted I was. I started to eat without thinking about whether what I was doing was right or wrong. The children were trying to find me, looking around, calling out; I stayed silent, chewing away at delicious delicacies. They were right: Armenian women were good homemakers and cooks.

When I had eaten to my heart's content, I emerged smiling from my hiding place because they hadn't found me and I had eaten the food meant for Mr Agopian. How cheeky children are, seeing life as a game. And really children don't live, they play, all is a game, they forget all their sorrows through games and laughter. They get happy easily, laughing over nothing.

Even as eighteen-year-old young women, we would laugh happily, we would sing like the birds, and the elders would tell us off, 'you are big girls now, young women, don't behave like that, people will talk'. That's how we lived back then with the Armenians: peacefully, happily and with love for each other.

That's what we thought

These people lived with their sorrow, the sorrow of the exile. They were refugees, immigrants, just as we are now here in Australia. It's only now that I can truly understand how they felt, to share their pain and to feel sympathy. Deep within me they have a place, a drawer with all the gifts of my younger years.

Next door to us lived Mrs Anna, Mr Socrates and their family: three children, the grandmother, and her brother who was single and lived with them. Word was that he was educated but worked as a shoemaker, that he kept in contact with his homeland which, at that time, was a region in the Soviet Union, and that he was longing to return to his country to be with his people; he dreamt of a free Armenia. He was always deep in thought, frowning and unsmiling. He only communicated with his inner self and with the agents that promised him passage back to his homeland, Armenia. He didn't talk with anyone, exchanging only the bare minimum at work.

Those seven people lived in that small house, composed of two rooms and a tiny kitchen. When I think back on it now, I wonder how they all fit; where so many people slept. It appears that Vanes, that was his name, was collaborating with countrymen back home, had kept up these connections, and was secretly working to return to his homeland. The whispering in the neighbourhood started to build up, coming first from the children, that the Armenians would be returning to their homeland. Their children, the little Armenians as we called them, were not happy at this prospect as they had been born in Greece, side by side with us, we had all gone to school together, we grew up together. In short, they didn't want to leave. They loved us, their friends, and they loved Aigion.

The women suddenly became serious, stopped smiling, didn't open up to the neighbouring women anymore. Some of the braver women amongst them confided that they didn't want another exile, that they had settled nicely into their little homes, their husbands were fine working in the paper mills – now that the war was over, were they to start from scratch again? How were they going to leave the friends they had made here? Where were they taking the children? Hardship and suffering all over again, a second uprooting. What news was this? We bumped into them on the road looking bitter. Mrs Maria had lost her beautiful curly hair, was crying and saying that she couldn't leave Greece as she had two children buried in the local cemetery. During the days of starvation, she lost two little children and she was constantly crying. But who listens to women? That's the fate of women, they have to obey every order given by the men. Our neighbourhood lost its joy, as though the landscape had darkened, enveloped by a fog, darkness. The women stopped gathering together in the afternoons, to chat, to tell jokes, to share their worries, to take heart in their children and in the small joys that each day brings. As for our friends, they too largely withdrew from our games. People were saying that Vanes was schooling them in what was to come, that they would be returning to their homeland where they would live a much better life, they would have their own country; they would be part of an independant country.

The Greeks in the neighbourhood also became preoccupied and serious, us children even more so. We were losing our friends, our routine. The atmosphere became heavy; everything around us became heavy and sad. They began their preparations, started selling their things and, slowly, their houses. What was going on? Us younger children, in particular, couldn't understand what exactly was happening. The Armenian women looked grave. Teary-eyed. One morning, the portentous moment of departure arrived. Commotion in the neighbourhood, a peculiar noise as though nature was weeping for her children who were uprooting themsleves, for our friends born here in Greece, in Aigion, here next to us, on the train line, where the whistle was our music and the train our toy.

Oh! How I loved those Armenian children, how I felt for them. I was devastated on the day of their departure, that moment of separation, young and old, all of us crying so much we couldn't let go.

And then came the silence, the pain, the grief. And then, one night, a light shone like a candle glow in our heart and mind. We had to let it go. Perhaps things will be better for them in their country. We consoled ourselves to lessen the pain.

Time, as they say, is a great healer and we grew accustomed to their absence, just as time set about healing us after other unfortunate situations, providing relief. And so it was back then. The neighbourhood changed, their homes were bought by others, we slowly got used to the new owners and grew to love them as well. We would often talk about our old neighbours, the Armenians, about their children, about our old friends that we grew up with.

Years ago when I visited Greece, I went to Souren's, the Armenian's, coffee-grinding store in Aigion and asked for information about our friends. Souren told me that they went through a terrible time upon their return as nothing was as they expected. He gave me Manoli's address. Manoli was my brother Christo's friend, who now lived in France. I wrote to him from Melbourne where I live. He sent me a reply together with a photograph that he and Christo had taken riding on a donkey.

He also wrote that he went to Aigion, down to the Line, and to the beach till the tip and all the way to Aliki, where we used to go swimming, during those beautiful childhood years. Oh, Life! How short you are, how strange but how beautiful … I don't know what happened to him after that as we lost all trace of our Manoli. He never wrote again. We always think about them and love them deeply and, now that we are also living in a foreign land, we understand them better. Because, despite the love that we had for them, the adults would here and there malign them, calling them 'dirty old Armenians'.

They used to say a lot of awful things, that they came and took our jobs, just like they said about us during our early years here in Melbourne. They used to call us 'bloody wogs' and our children were treated badly at school.

The golden years

The golden years, as we call the years of youth. We, too, experienced these unique, golden years. After 1950, when the civil war was over, people had a thirst for entertainment and happiness. Even us poor young people had good, joyful times. For, you see, young people find enjoyment in everything, they don't really care about financial difficulties.

I remember our group of friends, we were between sixteen to twenty years old, and would meet, chat, watch movies at the cinema. Back then, Aigion had two winter cinemas and one summer outdoor cinema as, the world over, movies were at their peak.

On Sundays we would always go to the cinema, no matter what, we would save money for the ticket, we would decide what movie we'd like to see and off we'd go all together. A movie played at the cinema in Anaplasi that I will never forget. It starred Brigit Bardot and when we got to the foyer the crowd was so large that, even to this day, I'm amazed that I managed to enter the theatre to find my friends. What can I say? Those years had a charm about them, a carefreeness and we would gape in wonder at the slightest thing. The adults would comment on this all the time, 'what are you gaping at like fish?'

The Haroni family also lived in our neighbourhood. They were quite well off, in a much better position financially than the rest of us. They had a store in the town centre, their house was tall and beautiful and they had only three children, Yianni, Leonida and Rina.

Well, Leonida would take the gramophone that they had in their house and would organise with our group, at one house or another, to have a party. And what parties! Dancing all night and no food, just a slice of apple or orange, that's all. Sometimes the lady of the house would treat us to some shortbread and then the party would become much more fun. At one of the houses, the floor wasn't smooth but earthen and had some fairly big holes in it. As we danced, we bopped up and down to the rhythm creating a scene that was so ridiculous, yet we just laughed and enjoyed ourselves even more. We didn't care about anything but having some fun.

Another time, Mrs Panagoula, treated us to some shortbread and left it on the chest of drawers. At each circle of the dance, my eyes fell on that shortbread and I devised a plan to sit next to it and grab a piece in a way that no one noticed. I never managed it, but I still relive that scene and that atmosphere with my beloved friends to this day. I always think of them, I yearn for them and they keep me company, tucked away in a drawer with the treasures of my youth from those beautiful years in my homeland.

My sister, who is a year younger than me, was going to high school at that time, but from very young children we were inseparable and we always kept company with her friends. Once, she said to me the night before, 'Litsa, tomorrow some of my girlfriends and I are not going to school. We're going to Koula's house and we're going to be all alone, because her family is from Diakofto, they just rent in Aigion, we'll have a good time, what do you say, are you coming?'

The next day five-six of us happy girls met to live a little differently, away from the glare of the adults. We felt that we were committing a sin because we were taking part in what was then considered truancy. And what were we doing? We were enjoying ourselves, talking loudly, laughing at anything stupid or any news that each one was talking about. How wonderful youth is! You feel happy with the slightest thing, with a glance at little things around you. As the song of singer-songwriter Daskalopoulos goes, 'Where are those years, those beautiful years, when you had flowers in your heart ...'

But let me continue with that day of our truancy. At some point Koula called on us girls to all sin together as she had some cigarettes! She lit a cigarette, tried to smoke it, gave it to the girl next to her and then all of us lit one up. I can't describe what happened next! The room filled with smoke, we started to cough, we were choking, but we were so happy, laughing, enjoying ourselves. It was the first time that we were putting a cigarette in our mouths and we thought we were so special, doing what the adults did. We agreed to never smoke again, though, as we didn't like it.

What we did like was going for walks up to the Ipsila Alonia area and gazing down at the Corinthian Gulf. My brother, Christo, loved Aigion very much and called it little Paris. It really was a beautiful town and it still is a lovely small town, combining mountain and sea, as do many other towns in Greece. Countless stairs connect the lower part of the town with the upper part, I can't remember how many there were, and we used to fly up and down them. We used to jump on those stairs five at a time singing, 'five by five these stairs I climb, come to me and please be mine …'

Now that I think back on it, I'm amazed that we didn't seriously hurt ourselves or break any bones, as mother would say. She would call us crazy kids and warn us that if we weren't careful we would kill ourselves on these stairs. Aigion was, indeed, beautiful, but it wasn't a little Paris because it didn't manage to keep us close, despite its many beauties. Lots of theatre troupes, touring the provinces, came to our town back then. They were referred to disparagingly, but they did present some fine plays, at least they seemed so to us. Singers would come as well and I remember a young girl who sang the songs of Atik beautifully.

I had seen Sophia Vembo and Traiforo as well as Vembo's sister, Aliki, a beautiful woman with blond-dyed hair, I had seen Eleni Hatziargiri, I had seen Nina, a tall, well-built woman, and many others whose names now escape me, but I do remember that I spent dreamy nights watching them. A glass of Vanilla-sweet in my hand, the so-called 'boat' or 'submarine', or a Turkish-delight, would last me all night. As for the poor venue, you can imagine how little they made. Difficult years, but beautiful years for us young people.

There were also beauty pageants: Miss Hellas, Star Hellas; we would argue about Haroula, Dezi Mavraki and Virginia Petmeza. We would all gather at Maria Papakonstandinou's house, establishing our own committee. We would nearly come to blows … That girl Maria was very good looking, nature having endowed her with many gifts, the greatest one being her voice. When she sang, as she often did, all the neighbourhood enjoyed it. She sang so beautifully that everyone said she could become famous. But who cared about such pursuits in those days. And so such a tender and, at the same time, strong voice, she didn't need a microphone or any other such assistance for her birdsong to be heard all over the Line, went to waste. Not like today when many girls who become singers can't sing but parade around naked to get noticed.

What to remember from those golden years! You'd be lucky to chance upon the parade that took place in Aigion the Friday after Easter when the whole town celebrated the Virgin Mary, or the flower festivals or when the high school ended for the year and the students descended on the Metropolis, making the tiles shake, what laughter, what joy, what beautiful young people, what beautiful years. They keep me company now that I live so far away from my country of birth. I keep them as a talisman, nostalgically recalling them, as well as my beloved friends, over and over …

Good dressing, swimming and flirting

Oh youth, youth where has youth gone, where has beauty gone, that they might come again. This phrase from the folksong says it all. The days of youth are the best time in everyone's life. Years full of joy, hope, questions and love intrigues.

At the age of eighteen, I was a new, young dressmaker, sewing the less important clothing for some ladies in Aigion, that is, over-dresses, blouses, not their Sunday best dresses in other words. The problem lay with the payment. It was so difficult to get any money from them and I had such a need for it. I had to contribute to my family's upkeep, give money to my father to help him make ends meet. I used to send my sister, Ioanna, to get the payment on my behalf as she was younger than me and couldn't very well say no.

She used to go to get the money that they owed me which, by rights, they should have given to me the minute they picked up their ready garments. But no ... Ioanna used to go and come back with empty hands. They would tell her to come back next week. Come next week, the same scene would play out. My sister felt embarrassed having to beg for this money and would refuse to come and go.

My poor father would pass by my workshop with heavy and hesitant footsteps, asking for some money to buy the essentials. As far as finances go, this was the situation but, despite all these difficulties, those years were the best days of my life. Years full of enthusiasm, love and hope for tomorrow.

However, with this skill I somehow managed to help my father and to buy lovely material for our dresses. We were four girls, all wanting to look our best, and everyone said that I sewed well (they say it to this day) and I made clothes for my sisters Sophia, Athina, and for our youngest one, Ioanna, who I couldn't get to sit still for her fitting. Silk, organza and taffeta were very fashionable at the time. I had even given the silk dresses to be embroidered by a woman expert at this craft who lived near the hospital.

The old hospital was a beautiful building near the market, surrounded by a lovely garden and was the pride and joy of the town. It has now become a cultural centre and the new hospital is in the upper town area, impressive as well, a modern institution. As I was saying, next to the old hospital lived the embroiderer who made a living through her embroideries. For you see, despite the poverty and unfavourable conditions, human beings crave beautiful things, fashion, cinema and stylish clothes.

Indeed, back then people really showed great taste and care in their choice of clothes. If you didn't look like a fashion plate you didn't step out the door. And I did sew well. Not because I want to boast but my sisters confirm this as do the photographs from this time.

I, myself, looking at these photographs, can't believe that I sewed all those clothes. Nowadays, I don't even sew a button.

My sister, Ioanna, says that it would be nice if I were to sew one good outfit a year for myself at least. But I can't. This job doesn't bring me any pleasure, I detest it. I worked as a sewing machinist for forty years here in Australia, bent over a sewing machine, I feel a weight on my back, I have hunched over, I can no longer stand this job. Back then it was different. I was young, it was a means to doll ourselves up, to go out. We'd say we were going out, meaning we'd get dressed to the nines, and go to the Psila Alonia, an outing where anything could unfold. Sometimes the theatre, other times the cinema, walking up and down, laughing heartily, secret glances with the boys.

It was customary on Sundays, after the midday meal, to have an afternoon siesta so that we'd be fresh for later. We'd roll our hair in little rags to make them curly. In those days curly hair was very fashionable. We'd wash our hands in lemon juice and we'd be ready to go out. On those outings, young people enjoyed whatever they liked, well not exactly, but, as I've said many times, the young back then were happy with very little. They just looked at each other, the flame of desire fanned by their eyes, the body would shake and tremble at this new-found bliss. The atmosphere was electric and we felt such pleasure the minute we saw the object of our desires. There's mine, we'd say; there's my girl, the young men would say. I had my eye, so to speak, on a boy from the outskirts of town and every Sunday I was anxious to see whether he'd come to Aigion. I was anxious about it all week. What years!

In summer we would meet up with our group of friends to go swimming, and I always suggested we go to Longos beach where that boy, my boy, lived (mind you, this young man had no idea about my feelings) although we never spoke, just exchanged glances.

My girlfriends realised what was going on and started teasing me. Come on, Litsa, let's go somewhere else for once, we're always going to the same place. What's so special about it? That's how it is when you are young, everything has a scent of honey and musk.

We also used to go to Saint Nicholas for swimming with my brothers, my sisters and our friends. My brother, Kostaki, had a best friend that he'd go everywhere with and we'd often go along as well. This friend, Vangelis, as I'm going to write about further down, had fallen in love with me as well, as these things happened back then, without ever telling me the slightest thing. Once he had brought a watermelon, he placed it on the edge of the sea, when suddenly the waves dragged it out. Vangelis ran and grabbed it. Yelling, laughing, the happy youthful outbursts of crazy young kids. We all gathered around sitting on the sand, Vangelis opened the watermelon and we enjoyed it amidst laughter and childish antics.

Now I'm going to tell you about the love that Vangeli had for me and yet never said a word to reveal how he felt. When I was living in Australia and was married, one day my husband brought in a letter from the letterbox, opened it and started to smile. Come on, he said to me, get ready to go on a trip, your boyfriend Vangeli is beseeching you to return to Aigion to marry him. My husband was smiling ironically, of course, but I was left with so many questions. With so many opportunities amongst our group of friends, on our outings, why didn't you find a way to tell me about your feelings, Vangeli? What can I say, those are the inexplicable things that happen to each of us.

I'm now writing about those years, about our youth, about those glorious years that we lived through when we'd feel happy over the slightest thing. Paradise was our garden. When I'd go to get water from the pump, I'd get so dizzy from the blossoms of the jasmine, the mandarin tree, the orange tree, the lemon tree that I would lie down right there under the shade of the trees and I'd feel wonderful. It was there that I wanted to experience love's passion. I've always felt a deep sorrow that my yearning for a young love remained unfulfilled. Now I recollect those years looking at the old photographs, at our beautiful dresses, the beautiful faces, and I still feel my heart skip a beat at the crazy antics, the laughter, the wonderful years of youth and the passions that were kept hidden …

Inner turmoil

I get confused by my homeland's figurines, harlequins with masks from another time, struggling with my identity.

I seek acknowledgement from my brothers and sisters, a little love, a seed from the pomegranate, to taste the freshness of life back then with you, mother Greece.

Yes, my life back then, when I walked barefoot without my feet bleeding or feeling pain because you were my mother, you caressed my feet with adoration, with love, because I was your child back then and you indulged me, sang lullabies to me, you would put me to sleep with the juice of wild grasses.

And I would sob for an apple, something tasty, a deprived child of the Occupation.

And yet I grew stronger with all these wild greens and began to dream.

To get the sails ready for the big journey, to make something of myself, to stop feeling like a worm, to start feeling like an eagle.

And so, mother Greece, I started asking for my share that you, shattered by your enemies, were in no position to give me. You had no morsel of bread nor a linen cloth for me in which to wrap my youth.

So! That's when I started an inner meeting with my insides, that had always bothered me, about the miserable life that I was offering them, and from this came the understanding that we had to set sail for another earth, another place.

Some of my insides and I agreed about this journey. Others didn't. And that's when the dance of protest began: wild voices, questions, accusations, they nearly drove me insane.

But my strongest inner-self protested and didn't want to follow, wailing, feeling dizzy, illnesses that stalled the journey, struggling, she couldn't tear herself away from her mother, sensitive heart, she felt for everything.

She loved everything, down to the little camomile bush that sprang between the stones in the corner of the house, she adored that too, now that the time had come when she must leave and become detached from all these beloved things in the house and in the homeland.

Our poverty-stricken homeland where we were sustained by the sun, her beaches and the surrounding landscape that makes you feel so wonderful.

But one night I found my other inner-self tired and I took advantage of its weakness, it was nearly dawn. I got up exhausted, went to the trunk where mother kept all our treasures and took a swaddling-band that she had been kept as an heirloom from the years when they would tightly wrap us up like mummies the minute we were born.

I needed it now to tighten my insides around my stomach and my belly, because I felt as though my body would come apart from the pain.

I tightened the sensitive part, washed myself, dried myself with the towel that ten people used every morning. I took my little suitcase and there I was, ready to raise the sail to reach my dream.

No matter how much it hurt, I had to follow it.

It went something like this

Forty-four years had to pass before I decided to write about my experiences from 1956 when I made the decision to migrate to Australia.

A lot has been said about the girls during the 1950s, 60s and later, who came here to marry a young man that had been recommended to them by a family friend or matchmaker, or those girls who had come here as maids sponsored by DEME the International Organisation for Migration. They were very difficult years and I feel that our country sold many of us off to lighten the burden on the rest of the Greek population left behind. After the war unemployment was high and poverty was rife. It was particularly difficult for a young girl from a poor family who had negligible prospects of some young man marrying her if she didn't have a dowry. There were no jobs, no prospects. Except for the rare exception of cupid's arrow hitting some ideal soul, a young man who was prepared to overlook everything, all the obstacles put forth by parents and society, and marry the girl in an attempt to win.

And so in 1956, since there was no light on the horizon for any work, no ability to make a living, I made the decision to migrate to Australia, after some intervention by some neighbours who had left as a family and had taken my photograph with them. At the neighbour's house lived young men who wanted to marry to have some financial support and to start a family. The dream of all young people, I think. One young man saw my photograph, he liked it and the usual began.

One afternoon, my father came home from the market and said, 'Here, my child, take this letter that Mrs Leta sent. Read it carefully and come to a decision on your own. If you don't want to go to Australia to marry sight unseen, don't agree to this.' I thanked my father and said that I would read it and make up my mind.

I reached out my trembling hand, took the letter and disappeared into the other room where we had a rickety old couch. I sat carefully on the end because the springs were piercing through and left marks, and started to read the letter. How can I explain what I was feeling at that moment? It would be very difficult for you to understand. Only the girls who were driven by necessity to migrate like I was could possibly understand me.

My mind and my whole being was beset by clashes and shuddering. Just when I would resolve that no, I will not leave my homeland to go to a foreign country to marry a man I have never met, I would change my mind. From my adolescent years I had created my dream. To get together with a young man that I loved, to build a house together with a beautiful garden surrounded by trees and flowers and our children playing, caressed by the rays of the sun, with me secretly looking at them from behind the window, admiring them. And in winter we'd all sit around the fireplace roasting chestnuts, with me making them pancakes and other delicacies with honey and sultanas, everyone looking happy, my husband and I enjoying our family, our love and our home. What happened to all of these dreams? How did it happen that this letter cast a shadow over it all, a grey veil over my dreams?

And yet, this couch with the broken springs and the environment generally, reminded me that I had to accept the decision to leave because there was no hope of settling down here, this was no place for innocent youthful dreams. I had to leave and help my brothers and sisters.

When I had talked it through with myself as much as I could and made the decision, I remember that I tried to seem composed and sort of happy. I came out of the room to tell my father and everyone else, as my whole family had learnt of the letter from Australia.

The decision

I would leave, I would go to Australia and create my future. From that day on, my life assumed a different rhythm, I saw, I felt differently, and no matter how much I tried to the contrary, everything came to remind me that I no longer belonged here but somewhere far away in the unknown. A myth of whisperings started around me, quizzical looks about my decision to migrate. Perhaps because at that time not many people from Aigion had left, from the surrounding villages yes, but not from Aigion. And so I was pointed out, there she is, Nikolopoulous' daughter who is leaving for Australia.

And I felt proud, satisfied that I would no longer live amongst them as a poor young girl. Other times, though, I would withdraw into my shell, overcome by sorrow and exasperation at the conditions that had impelled me to take such a huge decision to leave my homeland.

At any rate, the correspondence with Mrs Leta began, where she filled me in, and then with the young man who was destined to become my partner. I began the trips to and from Athens, fronting up before doctors, and I couldn't wait to get my visa to leave, I had grown emotionally weary with the whole situation and had lost weight.

The last time I was checked by the doctors, they told me to go on a holiday and to overeat to restore my health, and the next time they might issue my ticket. I got really upset at this. Those doctors understood nothing about me that they would give me such unrealistic advice. Where would I find the money for holidays and overeating?

No matter. I took the bus back to Aigion and leaning my head against the window, as I felt hot from the millions of feelings, somewhat cooled me down and I let my thoughts embrace the passing landscape that I would probably not be seeing many more times. I tried to store away in the drawers of my mind everything about my homeland to keep me company. When I reached home, my parents were worried seeing me so disoriented. The questions, from parents and siblings alike, began falling like the first rains and I couldn't keep up with answering them all. I told them roughly, not exactly, what had happened and that next time they would give me my ticket. Everyone calmed down somewhat and when it grew dark we withdrew to our beds for sleep. My sister and I didn't sleep that night. We stayed up talking and making plans. The next day I went to Lourida, to the dressmaker that was considered one of the finest in Aigion. I asked for work and she hired me. It was exhausting work but I was making money that enabled me to buy meat, eggs and milk to grow stronger. I remember once that I was ironing and feeling very tired. I started to feel dizzy and lost consciousness, falling right to the floor on to the rug. The dressmaker, Koula and her sister ran to revive me and then took me arm in arm to my sister, Sophia, who lived nearby.

Preparations

Despite the exhaustion, it seems that the good food did its job and I recovered from the weakness that my constitution presented. When I went for my medical tests again, the doctors found me well and gave me my visa. I returned to Aigion and the preparations began. To finish my embroideries, to sew a robe for inside the house, to look for patterns for silk night gowns with lace. My poor mother was weaving an intricate sheet but was pressed for time to finish it so we both worked at the loom. That's when I learnt to weave and I was mesmerised by the patterns and the colours. I enjoyed this so much perhaps because I knew that it was only for a short time. I remember that we went through so much to get a quilt made. My mother bought the wool, washed and prepared it ready to take to the merchant who would make it into a quilt.

Christo, that was the name of the young man who was sponsoring me, had sent money to get a quilt made because he wrote that it was very cold in Australia. I never used this quilt, it was unnecessary. It was heavy, coarse and, as the covering was silk, it was slippery which made it impossible to cover yourself. But I always remember what my poor mother went through laying the logs out in the north wind to heat up the cauldron, setting up the stands for the trough and washing the wool for this quilt from morning to night. So be it. No one can escape their fate.

Christo wrote to me, sent me his photograph, and I have to admit that I wasn't averse to him, he was nice. If I hadn't liked him, I wouldn't have agreed to marry him. Everything was prepared, a trunk with my dowry and a suitcase with my clothes and my books as I always liked to read.

Books always were, and still are, precious company to me.

I left for Athens and the great journey, accompanied by my siblings, Kostaki, Christo and Ioanna, together with friends from childhood. We reached the port and I didn't know what I felt. I don't think I truly comprehended that in a little while I would lose everything I loved, distanced from my parents, siblings, friends, and that I would find myself in the Antipodes, so very far away. When you are young, you have dreams and inner strength. You believe that everything will happen as you dreamed and planned in your mind.

My siblings and friends and I farewelled each other in a pleasant atmosphere I would say. They were all smiling and teasing me that now I would get to experience my every desire.

On the ship

I went up the steps as though hypnotised, some other force directing my movements, my steps and my whole body. I was following my fate. I leant over the banister trying to see my loved ones to wave goodbye to them. When everything was settled, they raised the staircase and the ship, the Tasmania, started to distance itself from the port and I could barely see my loved ones anymore. At that moment my eyes welled up, a knot formed in my throat and it was only then that I understood what a decision I had taken. I had turned my back on all the people I loved for the sake of finding work to survive and settling down. I started to wonder why our homeland or our politicians more to the point, weren't able to find another solution apart from this one where they signed agreements and sold us like sheep.

Now in this ship began the Golgotha for every young woman. In every cabin slept three or four girls. When I'd go down into this space I felt as though the end were near, dark, damp, exactly like a grave. I would go down only to sleep very late each night, avoiding being in that place as much as possible. I always sat on the deck, doing embroidery, reading, attending English language lessons and so the days passed. I had also made some acquaintances. There was a lady I knew from Aigion, with two young children, who was happy to reunite with her husband and I envied her. I had met her just before leaving when an aunt of mine asked me to help out with her children during the trip. I kept company with an elderly man, a wonderful person, well read, from Egypt. We exchanged books and when I disembarked in Melbourne, this good man gave me his address as he was continuing on to Sydney. But after all that happened from the minute that

I set foot in Melbourne, I lost his address and, inevitably, all trace of him. How I would love to see him again to have a chat.

The trip was very tiring and we even had a fire on board which caused commotion and sent us all into a mad panic.

We set out from Athens on 11 September, disembarking in Melbourne on 15 October. When they told us we had arrived we felt as though the hour had come for our revival. There was such a hubbub, pandemonium, yells, I felt as though I was in a battle, fighting to see who would win. I grabbed my suitcase and, as soon as I heard my name called out, headed towards the exit staircase.

In Melbourne

As soon as I stood on solid ground again, I saw Mrs Leta with her family and another person in the group. I immediately thought this might be Christo, although he did not resemble the image in the photograph he had sent. He had a lot of scars on his face, perhaps as a result of some accident. Mrs Leta told me later that he hurt himself at the factory.

Anyway, I followed in their company and, at some point, I felt a spark like an ember warming me. It was Mrs Leta walking with me, arm in arm, and I liked the feeling of having my own neighbour caring for me, here in the foreign land, in this unknown. We arrived at their house somewhere in Kensington. We left my things at the entrance and we went to sit in the dining room. Mrs Leta had prepared soup, adding egg and lemon on the spot, and we all sat around the table eating hungrily.

Mrs Leta then addressed me, 'Come, Litsa, tell us how your journey was coming over'.

'To be honest, even though the journey was tiring and in the middle of the ocean the ship caught fire and we nearly died of fright, we made a happy time of it. I had all the time in the world to read, embroider, go to English classes, help the lady from Aigion with her children, have lovely discussions with an elderly gentleman from Egypt. The food was ready, everything was ready, why should I complain? To be honest, because I often thought about things and didn't know what I was going to find here, I didn't want the journey to end.'

Everyone laughed at this and Mr Andreas who hadn't spoken all this time said, 'Come now, Litsa, didn't you have us here? Why didn't you want to reach your destination?'

Mr Andreas was a little strict in his estimation of things, as I was to find out later. He, himself, adapted to everything as long as he made money. He had been so deprived and was so disillusioned in Greece where he worked at rope-making and couldn't make ends meet, that everything seemed easy in Australia.

He looked at me over his glasses intently, at least that's how it seemed to me, and I was jolted into attempting to justify myself, worried that I had said something wrong that upset them. I explained that I only meant that the trip went well because I was learning English which I knew would be useful here and that's why I liked it. Then, just at this point of myth-making, Christo, who was sitting opposite me, beckoned to me to follow him to show me something.

We went into the room where I would be staying, where I sat on the very edge of the mattress, and he started talking. 'You know I've got a lot of money, I've got a house that I'm renting out'. He got up and from his back pocket produced a small little notebook and then said to me, 'Do you see this? This is a bank book, look at how much money I've got!' What could I say? So, I said, 'Bravo. If you've got a house and a bank book with a lot of money, you must be a hard worker.'

He said that he was, that his boss loved him and that tomorrow he would go to work as he couldn't miss a day. What could I say, at that moment I didn't even know where I was. I told him to do whatever he thought best. He told me not to worry, that out of so many tenants someone would be home the next day.

I got up and went into the dining room, longing to escape that atmosphere full of incomprehensible and nonsensical things, bank books, bosses, bags of money and the like. My mind was spinning. How is it possible that someone waiting for a young woman from Greece, with the prospect of marrying her, to say the things he just said and, at the end, to inform her that tomorrow he was going to work because his boss loved him.

I went into the dining room and felt better amongst the people I knew. Mrs Leta asked me about the neighbours:

'How is Alexandra? Is old Moustina still alive? How is Dionysoula's health; Is your family well? How is Ioanna? Is she still continuing with her studies? What does she think, will she also migrate and join you?'

'They're all doing reasonably well but you, yourself, know how your compatriots live, in poverty and wretchedness. And Mrs Panagiotaina, the widow, with the five children, it would be good if we could organise to bring Kiki and Parthena here to settle and marry because without a dowry such things are impossible in our homeland. As for my sister, Ioanna, she couldn't talk about anything else but that I should sponsor her the minute I could. Athina wants to settle down but there is no hope without a dowry and so, later on, she might decide to come as well. She doesn't want to migrate but, in the end, she probably will too, what can you do?'

'Litsa, I think you are exhausted from the journey and we've driven you crazy with all our questions. Let's all go to sleep because tomorrow we get up very early to go to the factory.'

I left and went to my room, trying to make sense of everything that had happened. The behaviour of my fiancé seemed very ungracious. Couldn't he think of anything else to say to me other than how much money was in his bank book?

I was thinking of all these things, trying to justify them when, just as the house was sinking into absolute silence, I heard a knock at the door, followed by a shadow nearing the bed. It was Christo. He sat on the bed and started to gesture that he wanted to remove the blankets.

'Come on', he said, 'Let's screw around.'

I sat up in bed, shocked at hearing his vulgar words.

'Please, what language is this? Be patient, we have a whole life in front of us. We're going to get married in a week, I'll be yours. that's why I came, I don't have anyone else here.'

'I want it now,' he said and I felt so shocked and humiliated.

I felt like I was going crazy. What words, what manner is this? Where are the dreams that I had about my life partner?

'Please,' I said to him, 'go to your room and let me rest, I'm exhausted.'

He left staggering, threatening me. All night I saw nightmares about someone coming near my bed that I found repulsive.

Couldn't he find some kind words to come close to me, to make me feel warm? Didn't he know that a young woman is a delicate flower and needs particular attention? Morning came and I was so exhausted that I didn't know where I was, I felt like a sponge that has been wrung out and is seeking a drop of dew, my lips were dry and the taste was very bitter.

In the morning, I got up and approached Mrs Leta, telling her about the scene that Christo created during the night and asking her to tell him to be more polite, that I didn't like the way he behaved towards me, that his words were ringing in my ears, making me dizzy. How could a young man, seeing for the first time the girl that he was going to marry, treat her in this way? His words and gestures were vulgar, how could I live with such a man?

I felt I was living a bad dream, that this couldn't be my fate after travelling for a month over the oceans to meet him. No, I just can't accept this. Mrs Leta listened to me carefully and gave me courage.

'Don't worry, Litsa, I am going to have word to him and he will not bother you again.'

'Thank you so much Mrs Leta. Please do what you can because his manner and behaviour have really upset me.'

As we were talking in the kitchen with Mrs Leta, the other tenants as well as Christo started coming in for their breakfast before heading off to the factory. During those years, two or three families as well as single men lived in the one house so that the owner could pay off his loan. The loans they took out were huge and there was no other way. The tenants saved up as much money as they could for a deposit so that they could also buy a house someday. Observing their life now, my head fell out of the clouds and landed in stark reality. At the offices of the DEME, International Organisation for Migration they had given us books with stunning photographs of gorgeous houses surrounded by flowers. Every young person who had migrated thought of these images, that's why they decided to emigrate in the first place, to get a job, to live honourably, and to not have the stress of how to make ends meet. During that first morning I started to come down to earth and to ponder these things.

The next morning

As they grabbed their bags in the morning, they all extended a kind word to me about not being scared, to be patient, and that they would return in the afternoon. Christo, downcast, without caressing me with a tender look, just said, 'Litsa, when I get back this afternoon, we're going to a relative's house'.

'That's fine Christo, as you wish, till the afternoon then'. All the while, the early morning hubbub was going on around us as they got ready to leave for work, with me looking on at their movements and faces, trying to make some sense of life in this new country that I found myself in. I heard Mrs Leta talking to me, giving me advice.

'Litsa, don't be worried, close the door after me and if anyone knocks, do not open. Have a rest, you're exhausted from the long journey over - when I get back in the afternoon we have a lot to talk about'.

With the last sound the door made as she left, the house fell into a strange silence, and I was overcome by fear, terrified, completely paralysed and couldn't understand why, like the wayward sheep that lost its way.

The day dragged, my mind buzzing with memories of home, praying to be near my loved ones again. I wasn't sure if I did the right thing taking such a decision to migrate to Australia to marry a strange man, wondering what was to become of me? What is going to happen to me with this man who comes into my room spurting vulgar language? How dare he talk about screwing around and then react furiously because he didn't get what he wanted. My God, who is this man?

I kept wondering how any man could behave in this way? Talk in this way? So cheaply, towards a young woman destined to be his wife? And at daybreak, when I so needed his company, leaving for the factory because his boss loved him and he didn't want to be absent from work and upset him.

I needed him now, today, he should have kept me company, we needed to get to know each other, to talk. How did he not think of these things and just left me on my own? These endless thoughts pressured my head, I wanted to no longer exist, to not have to live through this situation. And yet I continued living, the afternoon came, and they all started returning home, commotion, chores, chatter, each person had their own jobs to do, cooking, washing, someone went outside to clean fish so as to not dirty the sink. He was a bachelor and seeing him sitting on the ground in the backyard he looked a little funny; I wasn't used to seeing men carrying out these sorts of chores. One was doing the washing, the other was ironing his shirt, all of them were doing something. Christo sat at the table and opened some books that I couldn't understand. As he told me, he was learning English by correspondence. I sat next to him peeling apples. I pricked a piece with a fork and offered it to him.

'Have some fruit, Christo'. He didn't look up from his papers. I just heard the negative tone of his voice, hitting my brain like a lead weight.

'I have to read my lesson because I have to send it off. I don't want to miss a lesson; I've nearly learnt the English language.'

I sat there dumb-founded, with my hand suspended in mid-air like a statue. I couldn't think of a word to say to this unnatural male phenomenon that I travelled to be with to the other ends of the earth, who was going to become my husband so that all my life's problems could be solved. Why is this happening? How am I going to connect with him?

Anyway, on Saturday morning he took me to the city to start preparing, to buy all we needed for the wedding. If I remember correctly, we went to Coles where they had kitchenware. He bought two forks, two knives, two spoons and two enamel plates.

'That will do for us,' he said. I don't know where I found the courage to say:

'Christo, you told me that you have aunties here and that they are going to come and visit us. Wouldn't it be good to get more cutlery and plates so that we can offer them our hospitality?'

'No, no, that's enough, Mrs Leta has more if we need them.'

'All right, as you wish.'

He grabbed our purchases and we headed for the train. Throughout the entire journey we didn't exchange word, the heavy atmosphere pushing us towards antithetical thoughts.

I was thinking that he didn't take me somewhere to shout me a sweet, a coffee, to have a chat with me, anything to lighten the mood, but nothing, utterly mute … and I was drowning in questions.

Christo, for his part, was probably thinking about the money he spent and that he would likely still need to spend. We got home early and this made an impression on everyone as the questions started.

'For goodness sake, didn't you take Litsa to see the city, the sights of Melbourne? You didn't take her to a Greek café, what came over you and you left to come home so quickly? Really, Christo, you are so stingy with money. You don't know how to be happy. You've been given an opportunity to enjoy life and you are indifferent.'

Mr Andreas was good-naturedly teasing him, but Christo, sullen and moody, replied:

'You shouldn't talk because you came to Australia already married. We now have expenses.'

The truth is that from the first night when he behaved so horribly with those vulgar words, leaving me alone the next day to go to work, and now with this shopping and the knives and forks, the apple I offered to him and his indifference, his mute demeanour, saying nothing to the woman who was about to become his wife, all of these things showed me what I had to do. I couldn't marry and live with this man. I made my decision. I talked to Mrs Leta and she understood me and respected my opinion. In any case, she could see it, she was living it. Christo and I were not suited to each other.

However, Mrs Leta's husband, upon learning of my estimation of the situation, did not accept it with understanding. He felt that the wedding should go ahead and that we would slowly get used to each other. In any case, everyone in the house understood and supported me as they could see that we were not suited and that the wedding shouldn't go ahead.

The uncle

A distant uncle of mine, together with someone from Aigion, had learnt about my arrival in Australia, and one day there came a knock at the door when they came to visit me. They found me very upset as I didn't know what to do. I think my uncle came to an understanding with Mrs Leta, and the next day when everyone was at work they came and took me away. They took me to a lovely house in Abbotsford, that's where my uncle lodged, with a couple who rented out rooms to bachelors. And there began another circle of life. I found work, I washed and cleaned for the bachelors and for my uncle in lieu of rent, a deal that they organised for me. I did what I was dutifully bound to do as I felt indebted to my uncle for taking me away; thinking he had saved me. Unfortunately, Christo started to threaten me, menacing me that he was going to kill me for leaving him.

After living in this house for two months, my uncle rented another house on Johnston Street in Collingwood. We moved to the ground floor. It was a huge house and the front door never closed. My uncle rented the space below that had two huge bedrooms, a kitchen and dining-room and a bathroom. I slept in one bedroom, while my uncle slept in the other with another three young men. And this is when the drama really began. My fellow countrymen started to gossip about me. Imagine that, leaving her fiancé to go and live with so many men! What a woman of low morals she must be and who knows what she got up to on that ship!

Well-meaning people informed me about what was being said in the community and I felt terribly upset because, to be honest, I didn't agree with my uncle's decision to have me live in the same house as so many men.

It was only to be expected that there would be gossip. And as I found out many years later, my uncle might have been homosexual which is why he shared his room with other young men but it was hard to discern the truth amongst all the hearsay. I was such an innocent country girl back then that I would never have suspected my uncle's sexuality. I just saw him and the other young men as hard workers, striving for a better life.

In any case, my uncle was a good man and ran a fine household. He cooked delicious food, he shopped, he went to church, he lit the candle like the best housewives but I always remember him with a sad demeanour and his fingers were never without a cigarette. When we got home from work, he would make us a creamy hot cocoa and he always found a way to alleviate some of the stress of migration. He would organise a visit to our countrymen on weekends, or a trip to the Greek cinema which was incredibly popular during those early years.

The lodgers

On the first floor of this house, lived four or five families, two of them were Greek, one Italian, one Dutch, and a newlywed couple, George and Joyce. George was Greek; the young lady, Australian, and my heart went out to this girl over the way her husband treated her. He wanted to act tough and he often tormented her. I remember once he gave her bread and raw onion to eat and poor Joyce, who was an innocent girl, kept saying, 'it's too hot' and he would raise his finger and threaten her. 'We said that you would do whatever I told you to do!' would come his reply. His poor wife would swallow with difficulty, tears welling up in her eyes, incessantly drinking water. But let's leave all that for now.

The Greek couple was newly married as well. The young woman was brought to Australia by her brother, Nikos. At the places that he frequented, he met Grigori who was up from the country and wanted to find a wife. The two became good friends, Grigori often visited Nikos' home where he was introduced to his sister, the deal was sealed and they were married. Nikos had come to Australia already married and he had two little girls. They had rented a room on the upper floor and I would see them go up and down the internal staircase, morning and night. So many people would go up and down those stairs that it was impossible to keep count.

In those days I worked at a clothing manufacturing factory in the city and, because it was Christmas, I had taken work to finish off at home. I felt better sitting at the window seeing people come and go, feeling that I had company. During the Christmas holidays, a friend of Grigori's came up from the farm to visit his friend and to see if he could also find a young woman to marry. He wanted to make a life for himself in Australia, in Melbourne, because farm life didn't satisfy him. He caught a glimpse of me going up and down the stairs and he said that he liked me. He was attracted to me because I was pretty and hard-working and he thought to himself that this was his best opportunity to settle down.

'Adriana,' he said to his friend's wife, 'I saw a girl who lives downstairs and I like her. I want you to introduce us; I want to take her for my wife.'

'No way', she replied, 'I can't because I don't really know her. I just say hello to her and her uncle when I bump into them at the front door.'

This house was like a monastery, with a large entrance and huge internal staircase where everyone would meet, but this was usually as we were all rushing off to work so we barely spoke. A quick hello was about it and so the woman didn't know us at all.

He was persistent though. 'Doesn't matter. Just go and say you want a dress made and you'll slowly get to know each other, then organise to go to church together on Sunday where I'll meet you and you can introduce us.'

'Okay, okay, I'll talk to her uncle and we'll see.'

Things unfolded exactly as George planned. He was no country bumpkin.

And so there we all were at the church. As soon as the church service ended and I went into the courtyard with Adriana and Grigori they introduced me to their visitor.

George told me he was here for the holidays. He worked on a farm but didn't like it and wanted to live in Melbourne as well, which he would do as soon as he found a girl to marry.

I found everyone's stance towards me uncomfortable, my every instinct warning me about what was going to happen. I felt swamped by all these strange faces. I knew they were up to something.

That evening I didn't feel well in this huge house. I felt lost, overcome by fear all night and saw the light of day exhausted, reliving all that had happened to me from the moment that I stepped off the boat.

I wanted peace and quiet, I didn't want to get married, I wanted someone to understand me and support me during these difficult times.

But all my loved ones were very far away, back in my homeland, my parents, my brothers and sisters and all my friends. Here in this foreign land I had to become strong and find the solutions to my problems myself, and even then these solutions had to be sanctioned by my uncle. I had to do as he said because he was responsible for me now.

I started to wonder about my parents and brothers, who were so strict and made my life insufferable, 'Why did you look at him? What were you laughing at with your girlfriends?' and whose behaviour within the home was unacceptable. I remember once when my brother had come home on leave from the navy and told me to iron his clothes. I was a dressmaker then and was sewing bits and pieces. There were no washing machines back then and no irons and so it was a laborious process. I put his clothes in the wardrobe and sat at the sewing machine to continue my work. In the afternoon, my brother returned in great haste.

'Litsa, where are my clothes?'

As I was bent over the sewing machine, I replied, 'They're in the wardrobe.'

But it seems he didn't like my manner or the fact that I didn't get up to give him the clothes myself.

Within seconds I felt a hand slapping me and with one violent push I found myself on the concrete floor. My mother ran to help me up, all the while comforting me, reassuring me that my brother was just quick to fly off the handle. I felt wasted. There was much commotion in the house from his yelling and a neighbour even came over to support us.

He got dressed and left as quickly as he came, going in to town, angry at everything, especially at his four sisters.

All of these memories, and many more besides, came flooding back here in the foreign land and caused me much anguish. How was it that my family was not worried now about who I was looking at or what I was doing at the other end of the earth? Weren't they worried now about my straying and embarrassing them, as they used to say?

Just as I was managing to get over the first fiasco of my inability to communicate with my so-called fiancé, I was now faced with this, more problems with men. Adriana talked to my uncle about her husband's friend wanting to marry me. My uncle, tired of all the gossip that was going on about me, spoke to me saying that I had to accept the proposal and settle down, thereby relieving him of the burden. Everything was arranged for the following Saturday when we would all meet to finalise things. I was terribly hurt as I didn't want to end up with someone whose character I didn't know.

Although no one asked for my opinion, I gave it anyway.

'But why, uncle, do I have to marry someone that I feel nothing for? Why do we need to hurry? I'm finally free, I have a job, I might meet a young man and we can decide together about marriage.'

'What are you talking about, Litsa? What words are these? Don't you hear what is being said about you leaving your fiancé?'

I didn't insist anymore. I didn't know how to fight back anyway, and just let things take their course. Others are always in charge of my life, particularly men. I couldn't sleep all night. I felt pressured and that I was going to explode. I knew that I wasn't ready for marriage.

I must have dosed off at some point because I was woken up by a nightmare that disoriented me and I didn't know where I was, what country I was in. I got up as though wounded, I didn't want to live anymore. I was tired of always being pushed around at the whim of others. And yet I didn't have the strength or the means to escape this fate that I didn't want or approve of.

The days passed and Saturday came when we were to be visited by the couple and the prospective groom. My uncle was racing around in an apron cooking, cleaning, setting the table, worrying about getting everything ready like a good housewife. And he appeared to be enjoying it. I did whatever I could, moving around like a lifeless robot.

The time passed and our guests started to arrive. The groom had two relatives that he invited, and they all sat at the table. They started eating and drinking, talking about everything and nothing.

It seems that the groom was in a hurry because he addressed everyone, saying: 'We came here for a reason but no one is saying anything about it. I saw this young woman, I like her and I want to marry her. She seems deep in thought and I don't know if she accepts my proposal.' My uncle was sitting directly opposite me and he kicked my foot. I tried to compose myself and heard my voice saying:

'Since you all believe that this is what should happen, I accept.'

Oh, how overjoyed everyone was, raising their glasses and wishing us a happy wedding.

The afternoon passed in this strange hubbub, everyone looking so happy and with me wondering how they were incapable of sensing my tragic situation. No one was able, or perhaps didn't care, to understand me or my life's dreams. Where are those dreams that I envisioned under the orange trees, those dreams about love and being in love that I anticipated for so many years? My dreams just disintegrated, they clipped my wings and I feebly didn't resist. Why? My words have been stifled and I can't scream out that I want them to leave me alone, that I want to be free, that I can't stand being pressured. A lifetime in Greece and now here under the volition of men. And so began another chapter of my life.

Engagement, wedding at lightning speed

The following Sunday we went to the Greek cinema together with my uncle. George seemed ecstatic that he managed to find a woman to solve his problems here in the foreign land, that he would be leaving the country town to live in Melbourne. He left the next day to go and wrap up his chores, talk to his boss and return for the wedding and his future.

Everything gets found out, and so it was with my former fiancé. He found out that I was getting married and turned into a raging monster, saying he was going to become a criminal, get his revenge for the way I insulted him and how ashamed he felt when I left him. He sent word that he was going to kill me. My life started to become unbearable. I would walk along the street scared that I was going to be hit by a bullet. I was hoping it would happen quickly as I could no longer live with this anguish. The days passed and George returned from the country blissfully happy, seeing everything in a joyful and positive light. We organised everything and the wedding took place. Not just one wedding, but three. First of all, my uncle took us to sign some papers. He told us that we were now married. I later learned that this was a civil wedding. Then he took us to a Catholic church and a service was held there although I don't know why as we were both Greek Orthodox. Finally, the designated day arrived and we had the Orthodox wedding. I think my uncle was scared and so now he could really believe that we were married. He, himself, had grown tired of all that was being said about me. People had made out that I was a cheap woman. And why? Because I didn't marry the man that others had chosen for me. The man in question made no effort to gain my affections even though I had resigned myself to marrying him. It was his vulgarity that drove me away.

Anyway, about ten or twelve of us got ready and went to the church altogether, to the Evangelismos Church, where the wedding took place. We returned home where my uncle and I had prepared food for everyone. We ate and danced and everyone looked satiated and happy, particularly George. I was not at all happy, however, and I recall that here and there someone would remind me that today I should be jumping for joy, which just seemed ridiculous to me. How could I be happy when here, again, I was ending up with someone who didn't touch my heart, stir my feelings.

Everything happened quickly and orchestrated by others because it suited them. I was annoyed by a few things that took place during George's visit to Melbourne. We were visiting someone who was celebrating their name day. When the music started, my uncle took me up to dance. As he was swirling me around to the rhythm of the tango, I caught sight of George looking at me in a knowing way, poking his tongue in and out of his mouth as though he wanted to consume me. I didn't like this motion, and his behaviour generally. It disappointed me. On another occasion, we had gone to the cinema with my uncle, the three of us. As soon as the lights went down, George started with his old tricks again.

He slid his hand to the back of my waist, pulled down my petticoat, undid my bra and started touching me. I tried to discreetly pull away, seized up my body, glared at him so that my uncle wouldn't realise the embarrassing things taking place, but to no effect, he just wouldn't stop. All of these things alienated me from him. I felt bitter and couldn't stand the way my life was unfolding. Why such superficiality? What's wrong with men that they can't find some lovely, polite words, some good manners with which to approach a woman?

When everything had gone as everyone thought best, when they had eaten, drunk and partied, the wedding celebration ended and everyone went to their homes or, rather, to their rooms as back then immigrants lived in rooms. Even those who had bought a house lived in one room and rented out the rest. We also went back to our bedroom as George had become my husband in the eyes of the church and society. Because of the story with my ex-fiancé, the groom had a fixed idea in his head that I must have had sex with him. I kept telling him to please stop as I couldn't bear to hear such ungracious, ugly words.

After such a conversation and under such circumstances, you can draw your own conclusions about the first night of our marriage, a night that all girls wait for and dream about from their youth. You can also draw your own conclusions about how lucky and happy that young woman remained to the present day. The groom got up, satisfied as to the intact virginity of the girl, he got dressed and called to his friend upstairs to relay the wonderful news. His friend came down to the dining room and the teasing and knowing looks started, drinking beer and celebrating the event.

I was following the whole scene and was perplexed as to the way men thought about things. They couldn't understand that happiness and love are not dependant on this one detail. I was hurt and wounded because I could see the egotistical indifference to the feelings of the woman. And yet I was also taking part in this, living out my strange destiny. I didn't have wings to fly to escape, to sing, to live, to yell with rage and to send packing everyone around me. I was chained. Without realising it, I was trapped within a male yoke. That's exactly how I felt but on Monday morning I got up and got ready for work.

A married woman

In those years, in 1956, it was very difficult to find a job and, if you found one, you worked hard so that they didn't sack you. And from here on another chapter starts and, with it, another drama. As soon as I walked out the door heading towards the station, I saw my ex-fiancé looking at me with a fierce gaze. Once I got to the factory, I confided in one of the other women who knew my story that he was following me and that he had threatened to kill me. I returned home that night terrified. I was really scared. This situation had become a nightmare as he would be around glaring threateningly. One day there was a knock at the door and I was advised that I had to front up to Immigration. As soon as I got there, the questions started pouring in. I answered everything, tried to explain why I couldn't marry him and, with a pounding heart, waited for my sentence.

The official flicked through his books, a number of forms and then addressed me smiling.

'Don't worry, if you don't like him he can't do anything to you. Here in Australia, the government supports women.'

When we left Immigration I thought that everything was settled. I calmed down and slept well that night. However, the next day as soon as I finished work, there he was again on the opposite pavement, trying to frighten me by keeping his hand in his pocket. I was shaking all over, certain that a bullet would hit me, hoping that this whole tragedy would be over quickly. When I got home I found a letter from my family back in Greece and I became a little happier. I thought that they must have received my wedding photographs and were writing to tell me so. Once I opened the letter and started reading the contents I was stunned, I lost my colour and I had difficulty finishing it. George grabbed the letter from my hand and started to read it.

My former fiancé, my nightmare, had written to my parents saying that he would not allow me to live, that he was going to kill me and that they would soon be wearing black. I lost my voice I was so scared and I was so worried about the child I was carrying. My life was constant torment. Wherever I went he was before me or following me, he became my shadow, I expected the worst, I was trapped in fear's web and it was strangling my insides. I was so worried about my baby that I would go to the hospital all the time to get checked and, at each visit, they would ply me with medicines. Life became unbearable. He continued to watch me outside my house, threatening to kill me, mad with rage and all because I embarrassed him when I wouldn't marry him.

Gossip

At the factory I would hear the workers, who were also young Greek women who came as prospective brides on the ships, talking and criticising in the crudest language those young women who became engaged via letter but would not marry their intended. I felt so hurt because I also was one of them, but I didn't feel that I did anything wrong, like what they were saying that the girls got up to on the ship coming over, neither did I ever see anything untoward going on amongst my fellow-passengers. Why were they saying these things? Were they doing it deliberately to put me down? I couldn't live with that man due to this behaviour, even though I came ready to face a life with him. His words still hit me like bullets in my ears, poisoning my inner world.

Luckily for me, a new girl started work in the factory one day, the same age as me and, through conversations, it appeared that she also came over on the ship, Tasmania. This young woman was polite, she liked me, she comforted me and she said the loveliest things about me to the others. I had seen her during the trip over but we hadn't talked. I admired her as she was a beautiful girl and set an example as she embroidered, read, went to the English classes and was a quiet, courteous person.

One of the female co-workers said to her:

'So, were you really travelling over on the ship with Litsa and is what you're saying true?'

'Of course it's true. I'm not related to Litsa neither was she my friend as she didn't even notice me on the ship, hunched as she always was over whatever she was working on at the time.'

Her name was Chrisavgi and she admitted that she knew my ex-fiancé and that she would talk to him about stopping his slander and harassment of me. I was so moved that my eyes welled up with tears that, finally, someone said a good word about me.

'Come,' Chrisavgi said to me, 'don't worry because it's not good for the baby you are carrying.'

And that very night when I got home, I sat and wrote a letter to my parents, telling them not to worry and that everything would get better. It did, indeed, seem that the whole situation started to take a different turn.

The next day there was a knock at the door and there was a policeman carrying some papers, but smiling, asking me if my name was Litsa Gogas. My ex-fiancé was suing me etc. etc. but he told me not to worry because women are supported here and that, if I didn't like him, I did the right thing by not marrying him. Another kind word was being extended to me. The lawsuit was cancelled but Christo's presence continued to frighten me whenever he lurked around the pavement, threatening me. I was very relieved that the lawsuit was cancelled. I had never been in a courtroom and I found the idea very unsettling.

Anguish

As I said the idea of the summons unsettled me, as did the continued presence of my ex-fiancé every time I stepped out the door. Every night when George came home I would tell him that Christo lay in wait, threatening me, and that I was scared to go outside to go to work. This state of affairs continued even though, with Chrisavgi's intervention, I believed that Christo might calm down and so close this chapter of my life.

One Sunday my husband, George, went to church on his own as I wasn't feeling well. At the Evangelismos church back then, Greek migrants would meet up and talk about their concerns, they met other compatriots, made friends there, arranged marriages, that's where everything was solved.

That Sunday, out in the church courtyard, was Christo. George approached him and reasoned with him that the way he was behaving was not logical and that, as a man, he should have some pride. 'If Litsa doesn't want to be with you, you shouldn't want to be with her either. Why threaten her and tell everyone you are going to kill her? And if you do kill her, what's in it for you? You'll go to jail and destroy your life.'

It seems that this conversation with George, and with other kind and sensible people who knew me, gave him to understand that we were not suited as a couple and that he should stop treating me this way, particularly now that I am married and pregnant.

He made the decision to leave Melbourne. He moved to Sydney and I heard that he had married. I was so relieved about the whole thing, but I found this out much later.

The same thing all over again

While Christo had made his decision and was travelling to Sydney, yet another lawsuit by him came to alarm me. The policeman came to the door, delivered the summons to me, and left. The same thing all over again.

Closing the door, I started to think about my life from the moment that I decided to migrate for a better life, far from poverty, wretchedness, unemployment, far from the pressures of the men that I couldn't endure. And what ended up happening? Once again, men were telling me what to do and were tormenting me, poisoning my blood with the way they behaved.

The man intended for me was threatening to kill me because I refused to succumb to his vulgar requests and actions that first night after I had just stepped off the boat. Then, my uncle took me in, supposedly to look after me, but he very quickly offloaded me. It was decided that I would wash, iron and generally keep house for a whole bunch of men, in lieu of paying rent, because 'men can't do these things' as my uncle would say. So much was being said about me in the Greek community. They just stopped short of calling me a prostitute, although what they based this on, without knowing anything about me and my tribulations, I will never understand.

After all this, my uncle then decided to marry me off as soon as possible as he wanted his peace and quiet. The opportunity presented itself with the visitor on the first floor, since he had come to Melbourne to find a wife, to marry and have a maid at home and a partner in the finance department. This visitor found his solution in me. As for me, after having been through so much by resisting a marriage to a man intended for me by proxy found myself, against my wishes, in the same position a second time. Of course, I resisted yet again. I went to my uncle in tears, pleading as to how I could be expected to marry a man I didn't know. He had just come up from the country and I had no idea what sort of person he was.

Despite my efforts, I didn't achieve anything. The wedding went ahead and so I got married with bruised beliefs. I was at the mercy of a man who, just before we went to bed together on our wedding night, informed me without shame or reason that if I wasn't a virgin he would pack his suitcase and go back to the farm. As I took my nightgown off, trembling like a captured little bird in a cage, I secretly wished that I wasn't a virgin so that he would leave me. Yes, these cages belong to men, who else are they going to belong to? It's men that dominate us and govern our every move.

I was recalling all of these things. I was moving forward according to the wishes of my husband. I was pregnant, I was suffering, I was disillusioned with life generally, yet every morning I had to get up early and go to the city, sit in front of a sewing machine and work all day, whether I felt well or not.

Johnston Street Collingwood

Four-five families lived all together as was the norm back then, in a large two-storey house, to save money. We all used the same kitchen and dining-room and shared other areas. At the back of the house lived my newly-arrived sister with my sister-in-law. A family lived on the ground floor where my uncle also lived in a separate room, while another room was shared by three bachelors. I used to call this house the monastery. It had a huge entry hall and a circular internal staircase.

This house belonged to a Mr Antoni, but he didn't live there as he had other houses, had no children, just had his wife and his houses. He would often visit us and make critical comments. He would appear unexpectedly and, as I was in the habit of turning on the light when I got home from work, he was always on at me. Our room was dark and, with the light on, my life seemed more bearable. When Mr Antoni would see the light through the crack under the door, he would knock and as soon as I opened would say, 'Litsa, don't turn the light on during the day otherwise I will raise your rent.' And I would reply that I wouldn't do this again. But I couldn't live without turning on the light. As soon as Mr Antoni left and I could see him down the road from my window, my hand was on the switch for the bright light that would accompany the pain of my migration.

Let's talk a little about the other tenants. Near our room lived an Italian family with two children, Sam and Mario. Sam was an adolescent, while Mario was still a child of about eight, lovely and sweet. Mrs Teresa was a beautiful, kind-hearted woman, a good housewife, emotional and sensitive. Her husband was a well-built, hard-working man with a hearty appetite, who I don't think worried about anything else apart from his food. They lived in two rooms. The whole family slept in one of the rooms and in the other, if the door was ever left slightly ajar, you could see hanging from chairs an assortment of sausages, salami and anything else that you could imagine: potatoes, onions, capsicums, fruit, packed crates, as though they were going to open a shop. He might have been a good provider, as they say, but he was very stern and, if I may be honest, and we are never really totally honest, he actually looked fierce. I never saw him smile at his wife or children, or at anyone else for that matter.

In this house where we lived, several families shared the bathroom, the dining room and the kitchen which was very small, just a narrow space where each woman cooked in turn and, whenever someone needed something from the kitchen, whoever was in there had to step outside so that the other person wanting something could enter. Whenever this happened, all of us would spontaneously laugh. Everyone except for Bruno who was always sullen.

However, I will never forget Bruno's wife, Mrs Teresa. During moments of loneliness we would chat effortlessly. She was also a young woman, even though she had older children. She carried a pain in her heart and when we would talk about her childhood years in Italy and about an old love of hers, she would always finish the conversation in this way, with a bitter smile like that of the Mona Lisa: 'And now Litsa, this is the man I ended up marrying.'

I never understood why Mrs Teresa would tell me this. It was only many years later when I had lived through my own Golgotha that I understood the pain that she was talking about. After our chats came to an end, she would fill a bowl with chicken soup and offer it to me, with all the kindness and support of a mother. 'Here you are, Litsa, go and have this soup, it will do you and the baby inside you good.' She could see that I was pregnant in my final month and still working and she felt for me. I could never forget her and I hope that she is well, wherever she is.

Let's move on to the Dutch family that lived in the inner rooms. There were many members in this family. They had four children and the parents made six. Another gentleman lived with them who was probably a relative, at least that's what some said. People were saying lots of other things besides. The mother was tall, well-built, very attractive you might say. Her husband was slight, short, skinny as though he were stunted and sickly. How could he ever cope with so many children and such a robust wife.

The other tenants had a lot so say, namely that the three adults were in fact a 'trio'. Who knows? The gossip about them was raging. The Dutch woman was constantly cooking lots and varied things, food, sweets, creams and stewed fruit. Whenever she was in the kitchen, lovely aromas filled the house. I so wanted to taste these delicacies but she never offered me anything even though I was pregnant and it is customary to offer a pregnant woman something to eat. Most of the time, this woman was in the kitchen cooking or in her room with the other gentleman, while her husband was at the factory working for a wage. And so the other tenants had a lot to say about this. She also didn't look after her children as she should, or at least that's how it seemed to me.

The eldest son was around seventeen and it looked as though Spring had awoken in him; he had relations with a young girl his own age. One day at the entrance where most of us would meet he approached me saying, 'Mrs Litsa, please would you wash this shirt because on Sunday I am going to meet my girl.' The boy used to go to some Christian gatherings and that's where he met his girlfriend. I said that I would and that his shirt would be ready by Sunday.

The shirt must have once been white but when he put it into my hands I saw that it was so dirty that it had lost its colour. Be that as it may, I put it in the sink, I washed and re-washed it, left it all night to soak and then scrubbed it again in the morning till it came up white. I ironed it and then gave it to the young man whose face lit up when he saw it. He was so happy that when he got ready in the evening to go out with his girlfriend, he knocked on the door and when I opened the young man looked unrecognisable, clean, well-dressed and he was even wearing a tie. He came to thank me and he radiated light and youth.

The tenants in the rooms changed often, each trying their best to buy their own home. The Dutch family moved on and a young Greek couple moved in. Anthi was from Mykonos and Andreas from Cyprus. This couple didn't have children and never had any. They were both well-built and Mr Andreas had no other concern but how and when they would return to Cyprus. He and his wife would often disagree about this issue. He wanted to return to Cyprus, she wanted to return to Mykonos.

Many years later they did leave but I'm not certain for which destination. There is no question that Mrs Anthi would have followed her husband to Cyprus as it was always the custom for the wife to follow her spouse, the more powerful gender back then.

Life in Australia in 1956 when I migrated here was very difficult and tragicomic I would say. As I said above, one person barely fitted into the tiny kitchen and yet several families all cooked there, often almost concurrently as during the day we were all at work in the factories. Often, one wife would have to cook quickly so that the next wife could begin her own dish. The same with the dining room; we took it in turns to eat. I will never forget the large Dutch family together with the gentleman who lived with them. Everyone connected him to the family as it appeared that he was in charge of the finances, at least this is what the gossip suggested. They organised it so that they were the last to eat in the dining room because they took a long time. They had an abundance to eat at dinner, followed by sweets and fruit, where as the rest of us ate one meal which we finished quickly. Let's leave them now as they had a good time of it in their own way.

All these years later I still remember George and Joyce, and how that domineering Greek tormented his poor wife. As I have already mentioned, the house was as huge as a motel, many families lived there but no one had the responsibility to clean the communal areas. No one ever swept that huge spiral staircase because the truth is that you would have needed hours to sweep and mop it, and we were all so tired from working overtime.

The landlord and his wife lived elsewhere on their own. They had no children. He would come by daily, not with his wife though, to check on the electricity usage, to get the rent money and to make critical observations.

One day he knocked on the door and, when I opened, there was Mr Antonis with a bouquet of flowers and a smile, inviting us to dinner at his home. At some point we managed to find the time and went over to his house.

His wife was of medium height and weight, a good, unassuming lady, who looked down to earth and devoid of worries, happy with her lot. When she had offered us something to drink, and we had talked about one thing or another, Mr Antoni informed me that I should tidy up the house, sweep the entrance and the staircase. I wonder why I, a pregnant woman, would agree to clean the house without payment? I now realise that I was very naïve to accept such a thing. One day, as I was cleaning the staircase, everything around me darkened and I fainted.

In those early days, immigrants formed close bonds amongst themselves and we all visited each others' homes. For relatives, friends, acquaintances this was our entertainment. This is what happened the moment I fell. Our friend Panagioti Fildisi came over and found me on the floor. He revived me and helped me get back to my room.

When George came home, they discussed the situation and organised for us to leave that house. We went nearby to Mr Stefano's house in Keele Street where my maid of honour Vasso had rented. The landlords, Stefano and Meropi, were a rather strange couple, very good homeowners, everything was clean and tidy, although they were a little cold and people of few words. We rented a room and were allowed to use the kitchen at will, but were not permitted to use the kitchen cupboards. All our belongings and foodstuffs were housed in our bedroom! This couple, who didn't have children, were trying to make money so that they could return to Greece, and we learnt many years later that they managed to do so.

And so with my koumbara Vasso, both of us new housewives trying to establish ourselves, we decided to make a traditional grape spoon sweet. We took the grapes off their stalks, washed them, added sugar and water and put it all on to boil. We suddenly remembered that our mothers also added blanched almonds. So, off we went to the neighbourhood shop to buy almonds. Like diligent housewives, we locked the house in case of theft and set off for the almonds.

We were chatting happily that in the evening we would be offering our husbands a spoon sweet. We finished our shopping and returned home. As soon as we opened the door a burning smell hit us. We headed towards the kitchen and what did we see? The stove was covered in syrup that had overflowed onto the floor.

We were stunned initially, not knowing how to handle this. We tried cleaning the stove, but everything was sticking to everything else just like the story old ladies tell children about the honey that was eaten and that made everyone stick together, old people, chickens, the rooster, the dog, the lamb and anyone else who came near to taste.

We finally boiled water and with immense effort managed to clean everything. We had to leave everything spotless, without any trace, because God help us if the landlords came home and cottoned on to what had happened. We would be looking for another house again.

We remember this incident whenever my koumbara and I meet up. It still makes us laugh and we always say that us older women should be very careful with our daughters and daughters-in-law. Young girls can't possibly be expected to do things as we now do them, after our many years' experience. With patience, a smile and love, everything is doable …

Our first house

After gruelling work and budgeting we saved up a small amount of money, a 'deposit' as they called it, got a loan from the bank and were so happy that we were going to live in our own home. Once we'd found it, not far from where we were renting and not too expensive, one afternoon George took us all to see it. It was in Keele Street, Collingwood, not far from Johnston Street. I don't remember the exact address, after so many years my memory lets me down sometimes. I could go past there one day to see the number, but I shouldn't complain as I'm 80 years old and writing my seventh book so I'd be ungrateful if I complained.

As I was saying, after work one day we went to see the house we were going to move to, our own home. All of us went along: myself, Panagiotis, Angeliki and my sister, Athina, who had that year come out from Greece. Once again, my mind is playing tricks on me. I can't remember if my sister Ioanna and Vasili were living with us or if we were busy preparing for their wedding. I'll check the details with Ioanna who types up and edits all my Greek-language books and who remembers everything, and with Vasili who has the best memory of all of us – nothing escapes him.

As we approached the house, George was beaming with joy.

'There it is, there it is, do you like it?'

'What's there not to like, George? You're going to become homeowners and stop paying rent. We're all ecstatic!'

The house was single-fronted, part of a line of similar terrace houses all in a row like siblings.

'Come on I'll shout you all a beer,' George said.

Panagiotis reminded him that he would have many expenses from now on, that he'd have to be careful with his spending, as a huge debt was hanging over him.

George told him not to think like that; that with hard work and careful saving all would work out well. We would be moving on Monday. All the banking was organised. Us women started to pack up our few belongings, and on Monday we moved to our own home. How happy we were! We started making plans as the house needed a lot of work: the kitchen was dreadful and many other things urgently needed attention, but most of them remained just that - plans. Anyway, we went to a second-hand shop and bought a bed, six chairs, a table and we were overjoyed with these things. People are a mystery! When you are young, I think that your mind has other dreams, you don't care about money, even though we needed to buy so many things.

In any event, we enthusiastically settled into our new home, but what 'new' home am I talking about? From the very next day we became aware of issues and, for us women in particular, there started a lot of difficulties and hardship. It had three bedrooms and in the middle was a room that could be used as a kitchen and dining room. But we were so upset to find that it did not have a sink for the dishes.

We had to lug our dishes out into the laundry, into the laundry trough, the whole space just a rough square concrete box. We had to be very careful when we washed the dishes, placing first a large plastic basin in the concrete trough as we washed our clothes in it; even though washing machines were available back then, we didn't have one. From what I recall, this was the greatest challenge, more of a hardship for us women, particularly during bad weather.

So many years have passed since then and yet Ioanna and I still wonder why the men couldn't have built a kitchen sink in a corner somewhere as there was space to do so. But what was the point? At the time we thought that we would soon buy another, better house.

In any case, George decided to demolish the fireplace in our bedroom to give us more space. He even brought in a compatriot of his that he called 'master-tradesman'. He ate with us, drank and laughed with us, we had a great time, we paid him well but at a discount rate.

I can't describe what went on that day when they started to demolish the fireplace. This man didn't have a clue about such matters, neither did George. They started demolishing the fireplace from the bottom up and they nearly, I mean nearly, caused the entire ceiling to collapse. Noise, dust, cries and chaos, lack of communication between them; they didn't know what to do. After a lot of hard work and much effort to think things through, the fireplace finally fell without too much damage. You can imagine how the room looked after all this and so it needed to be painted. I don't know what came over George and he bought red paint. He painted the room red.

I got so upset about this but, no matter how much I begged him to change it, I didn't achieve anything. And so there I was in the red bedroom. I slowly got used to that too. He had a little bit of paint left over and decided to paint the kitchen chairs red as well. And on the façade of the house, George painted some beautiful flowers and was so excited. He would say that our house was the most beautiful in the whole neighbourhood.

The red chairs

While all of this was going on, Ioanna was getting ready to marry Vasili and the rest of us were thrilled about it. This was because Vasili was from Aigion and we met him when I came here to Melbourne. He was a good friend of ours and many Sundays, just about every Sunday, he would visit us together with Spiro Vagenas. We would eat together and would talk for hours about, what else, Greece and all we left behind. Spiro Vagenas was also from Aigion but he had the misfortune of being seriously injured in a railroad accident. He had no relatives here, and so Vasili, my husband and I looked after him. Vasili had assumed responsibility for his welfare, was his protector.

This was a difficult situation that caused us immense sadness. When he recovered a little, he left for Greece. He also went to Russia to have major surgery. He survived in the end, although he had trouble walking and with his speech. Even so, he married and had a family and actually did well financially. As I was saying, they were our good friends and when Ioanna migrated to Melbourne, they came to welcome her and for Vasili to get a package that his parents had sent over for him. That's how they got to know each other. They would go out together sometimes as, being from the same Greek town, they had a lot to talk about. They developed feelings for each other and decided to get married.

We were ecstatic about it because here in this foreign land this was something beautiful to see within the reality of the times. We were excitedly preparing for the wedding and a happy George decided to paint the chairs with left over red paint to make our kitchen look nicer.

We got together for the wedding, about fifteen people all in all, including the couple. The relatives, the best man, the two little flowergirls, Eleni and Alexandra, Vasso and Thanasis, our own best man and woman, and one of Ioanna's co-workers from the Phillip Morris factory.

When we got back from the church, we happily sat around the table that we had prepared for the feast. In fact, only the newlyweds and the men sat at the table. The rest of us women stood around looking after them. In those days, I remember we used to drink beer and wine. The red chairs went down in history! We still laugh about this today.

It seems that the groom, Vasili, had perspired, the chairs hadn't dried properly, and the sleeves on his pure white wedding shirt attained Picasso-like patterns. When we saw the damage done, we all started laughing and teasing Vasili and George in turn, the latter for his craftsmanship and the red chairs. Vasili said that here was a tourist groom with a multi-coloured shirt. He continued teasing that when he and his wife were able someday to go to Greece for their honeymoon, he himself would wear that shirt as it would be perfect.

There's more to this story. The next day when Ioanna went to work at the factory and the other women asked her how the wedding went, she told them about the shirt. One of the workers, Betty, advised her to clean it with acetone that we use to remove our nail polish. And so the very next Saturday when doing the laundry, our dear Ioanna decided to apply this method and clean the patterns off the shirt. She placed the shirt flat on the table and started rubbing it with acetone to get the red paint off. The funny thing was, however, that the table was covered with a piece of linoleum with a pattern of flowers and twigs on it and the shirt, instead of getting cleaned, emerged as a printed fabric with the patterns of the linoleum.

After all of this fuss, the shirt went to the corner of some drawer. Ioanna told me that she eventually made a little jumpsuit out of the good bits for Vicki, their first child. We laugh about this incident to this day. For you see, when you are young, even during hard times, you find ways to enjoy yourself.

I am nearly due to give birth

As my pregnancy advanced and I was in my last month the women around me, and even the men, started to tease me saying, 'For goodness sake, Litsa, are you going to give birth on the job and put the baby in the box with all your other finished sewing pieces?' I just lowered my head and said that I had to work, that I had to help my husband save for a deposit on a house. At some point, however, my body gave way and I fainted. When they had given me first aid, they called a taxi and sent me home.

That evening when George came home from work, I told him what had happened.

I explained that I wasn't feeling well, that I couldn't and didn't want to go back to work, that I felt embarrassed at what my co-workers were saying. And what did my good husband, George, reply? 'Let them say whatever they want. You go back to work and don't care what they say. Act as though you don't care.' I couldn't believe my ears when I heard these words. How could the man who married me so that we could have a life together, to have a family, not care about me, not understand how hard it was for me to sit at a sewing machine all day, suffering in the last month of my pregnancy?

And so I went back and forth to work until the day, in the tram, when I broke out into a cold sweat, was beset by unbearable pain and, instead of going to the factory, went to the Queen Victoria Hospital, and it was there that in the afternoon I brought a child into the world, a new life. That night I was told that when George returned home, learnt that I was at the hospital and that I'd given birth to a boy, that he glowed with joy. What a wretched state of affairs this is, that women are always in second place. It is women who have the most peaceful sentiments, make do with everything, make everything more beautiful, even calm down raging passions.

A woman will sacrifice her life for her family and yet just about all men long for a son. And I'm certain you all know, as I do, of cases where husbands didn't go to the hospital to see their wives who had given birth to a daughter. When these poor women returned home, the husbands wouldn't talk to them, treating them like maids, outrageous behaviour. What can you say …

I also want to highlight the things that happened during those early years of migration when so many young women came to this foreign land to marry a stranger who wanted a wife to solve his problems. This whole situation arose out of families back in Greece wanting to lighten the burden of their daughters because of the huge and never-ending problem of the dowry system. Here in Australia the women brought home a weekly pay packet and so there was no issue. Mind you, many young women were not even allowed to open it. Most women were promised, I could even say 'sold' to a particular individual that they had never seen and who didn't resemble the photograph sent.

Any woman who resisted this fate was made out to be a prostitute. But I have a pressing question here. How is it that the parents and brothers of these women, who made their life a living hell back home, who didn't allow them to have relations with other young men, forbidding them to smile or talk to them, who would get furious over any suspected misdemeanour saying that it would bring shame on the family? The brothers, of course, would go out all night and have a great time because they were men, you see, the madness, the egotism, of men. So, to get back to my question, how was it that when their daughters and sisters got on those ships they didn't care where they were going? They didn't care who they were going to meet? They didn't care about what would befall them?... But, of course, now those young women were far away in Australia, out of their immediate circle, they didn't have to worry about them. I, myself, now belong to another man who governs my every move. And yet, although he governs my spoken word, has no power over what I write.

I want the things that I write to one day see the light of day, to be published. I want my children to understand that if they now live well, choose their partner, go on a honeymoon and live a better life, that they should not forget that their parents underwent years of hardship here in this foreign land. Those young women, who left their homeland and came here for a new tomorrow, often came up against such a lack of understanding that they were driven to despair, even suicide.

It is to these wounded, immigrant women that I leave this book because I am one of them and I always think of them with love and compassion.

The house of joy and sorrow

Even though we lived for a short while in our first house in Keele Street with the tragicomedy of no kitchen and going in and out of the laundry, summer-winter, to wash the dishes, with the red bedroom, with the artwork from the red chairs that painted Vasili's wedding shirt, we have our memories that find their way into this writing.

Slowly, after copious budgeting and doing without every luxury, young people today could never comprehend the harshness of our life back then when we, ourselves, were so young, we managed to save up a deposit, secured a loan from the bank, and started looking for a better house.

George sought the services of an agent whose office was in Collingwood. This gentleman was Italian, handsome, well-spoken, down to earth and kind, trustworthy. At least, that's how he seemed to us. George chose him because he told him that he was experienced and, given that he was also a migrant, understood our situation.

He would take George after work to see some houses that were for sale in numerous areas, but George wanted the house to be near public transport because we didn't have a car to get to our work.

One sunny morning, it was a Saturday, the agent took George to see a small house somewhere in Northcote that was for sale. It was small, single fronted but was on a beautiful allotment. It had glorious flowers, a huge mulberry tree, lovely swings for the children and a large, new garage.

I'm not quite sure as to how it even happened, perhaps because George's English was not so good as to know the laws of Australia and the underhanded tactics of real estate agents, the latter convinced us to buy the house, citing it as a great opportunity. The owner was in a hurry to sell because he was leaving for Hungary. As I said, the house suited us, it was close to transport, was carpeted, had curtains, a kitchen that we had never experienced before, a lovely dining room and was beautiful overall. What an opportunity, given that we didn't have the money to buy these lovely things that a house needs.

Once we had sold the old house the date came when we had to move out so that the new owners could move in. We moved into our new home. All of us were happy.

Really, what happiness it is to own your own home, to enjoy the garden and to take pride in your children playing on the swings. When we had finally settled in and just as we were feeling that luck had favoured us in this foreign land, one fine morning came a knock at the door. There stood a stern looking man with papers in hand asking us why we were so late in paying the instalments for the carpets, the curtains, the dining table and chairs and the garage. We just stood there mute, the earth gave way under our feet. We told him that he must be mistaken, that we hadn't bought anything from him, that we had recently bought the house and just moved in.

'No, madam, such and such a gentleman bought all these things on credit and if you don't pay for them, we are going to come and take them.'

'But we paid more for this house because it was furnished.'

He insisted, shaking the papers before us, saying that if we didn't pay up by a certain date, they would come, rip everything up and take them away. Otherwise, they would take us to court.

When he'd left, we drowned in our sorrow. We couldn't breathe, couldn't move. The drama began with papers arriving about having to present ourselves in court on a certain date. George represented himself in court as there was no money for lawyers. I insisted that I wanted to go as well. I wanted to have my say, to explain what had happened, but George said no, as we couldn't afford to lose two days' work. I felt wounded, as though being shot at by the Germans with a bullet lodging in my back.

That night when George got back from the court I was dying to learn what had happened, what the verdict was. George was devastated, saying that we lost the court case and that they would be coming to take the things away. What can you do in such circumstances? We just got on with our factory routines and the thousand questions we had about this family drama.

I couldn't sleep at night and just kept asking myself over and over: how can people go into such debt and then just disappear? We tried looking for the previous owner but soon found out that he had left Australia and the police couldn't find him anywhere. My thoughts also turned to the agent who sold us the house knowing full well, I have no doubt, that these items were owed but who couldn't have cared less about our predicament. All he cared about was his own self-interest at the expense of people who didn't have the means for legal representation and gaining justice.

Anyway, on the appointed day, three workmen show up with papers in hand and, with their tools, started what seemed to me to be pillaging. They took down the curtains, took away the dining setting and, with their hammers, started ripping up the carpet. With the noise from all these tools I felt like going mad. With my child in my arms I would go from one room to another so that I wouldn't bear witness to the horrible things going on. Then they went outside and dislocated an entire garage. They loaded it onto their truck and off they went.

Such a silence fell, after all those banging noises, that I didn't know where to go and what to do in this bare house. With my child in my arms, I stepped outside, sat under the mulberry tree and let my tears flow to appease my soul. My child looked up at me with concern. My precious little one was too young to understand the drama and pain suffered by migrants.

With the passing of time, and after talking with people who knew the English language, we found out that they had no right to rip up the carpets and the garage because the law forbids anyone taking items that are nailed down in a property you have bought. Be that as it may, we suffered much torment in the early years of our migration. We suffered greatly and others suffered even more, but we emerged victorious. We established good families and we are now writing about it. If our children and grandchildren read about what we went through, it is a cautionary tale for them to be good people, fair with others, because when people behave in a just, empathetic and honourable way humanity as a whole is the better for it.

Our second house

No matter how many worries we went through in this second house, we also had times that were joyful and very moving. When our youngest child was five-months old I decided to work from home. I would sew swimwear as well as jackets for the snow. I didn't have a sewing machine but I found out that a factory that was close to our street gave out work and provided sewing machines.

I organised everything, that is, that they would bring me a sewing machine and provide me with work, and would pay me per item finished. What can I write about this? Whatever I write, I could never convey what this experience was like. Now that I recall scenes from that time, I am amazed that I survived this insufferable situation.

They brought me the machine and a box full of clothes to sew. We put the sewing machine and the box in the bathroom that was huge and that we used for many other things besides. That bathroom had become my nightmare from the arduous work but, most of all, the hot water heater that was next to the bathtub. As my older readers will know, in those days you lit the water heater with a match and every time that I lit it to bathe the children the gas made such a racket that you thought it was the end of the world. It made such a loud noise that I could feel my body disintegrating. I can't describe the feeling in words.

It was in this bathroom that I started to work for my daily dose of trauma. This was because the sewing machine they brought me was old and damaged. Every few centimetres it would cut the thread and it felt as though my life was being severed, and my daily paypacket. We didn't have a telephone and so I would go a little further down the street and beg the family there to use their phone so as to ring my boss. They would send someone to mend the machine but after a while the same thing would happen all over again. I didn't know what to do. One day I set out for the factory where I asked to speak to the boss.

The boss was a woman and she seemed cold and haughty. My voice was breaking but I pleaded with her.

'Please, you're a woman. I hope you can understand my plight and help me. This situation is so unfair. Please give me a good sewing machine so that I can do my work. The way I'm going I can't make a living because the thread is constantly being cut. I need to work, we owe our house and have so many other debts, we've had a lot of difficulties and setbacks.'

And I have to say that this boss or manager, I'm not exactly sure of her title, gave me her word that she would send me a better sewing machine, and she did. And I continued living the horror of this piece-work in the bathroom which doubled as my workspace. The work was incredibly hard because if I deviated one millimetre in the stitching they would send it back to be redone. These were difficult times.

It was during these times that we, five brothers and sisters, decided to bring our mother out from Greece. The trip was organised once mother decided to make this long journey at her elderly age. Our joy was indescribable that we would be reuniting with our mother after so many years apart. We had lost our father, who had died from heart failure. Mother was on her own and she made the decision to come and see her children in the foreign land. The day arrived and there we were at Port Melbourne to greet our mother.

Anxiously waiting on the platform we suddenly see our mother, tall, slender, elegant, with her hair in a bun and with glasses, with her careful gait. She was always beautiful, even in old age. Mother always had a problem with her eyesight and walked slowly, carefully, and that gave her an aristocratic air and charm. She was a beautiful woman and was famed for her beauty.

When she came down the stairs and we were together again there were hugs, kisses and tears. Joy, deep and silent emotion. Mother was bending down, not knowing which grandchild to kiss and hug first. We went to my house because that's how she wanted it, as I was the first to leave for Australia in 1956, and I had my little boy, Panagiotaki, who was named after my father.

Here in Australia we call Panagiotaki, Peter. When we say this name in the Greek language it sounds like the word for pie, Pita, that we bake in the oven. My mother would say, 'Why do you call the boy this? What a silly name is this? Is he a pie that we eat!'

***

During those years we also had some happy times. It didn't matter whose house mother stayed in because every night we all got together in one house or another and life was much more pleasant. We also had some sort of outing every Saturday, whether a wedding, a christening, a birthday party, we would always go somewhere despite the hard work we carried out. We managed to fit everything in. We were young back then! Young people can do anything! Now that my youth has passed, I think about those years, our good years, I never gave a thought to the fact that they were passing, never to come again.

In this house, in this neighbourhood, at 20 Northcote Street, Northcote, we experienced and continue to experience good days. Back then, our children played freely on the road and we would take them further down to the beautiful park on the corner where they could be carefree and play happily. There were no cars back then and we could proudly watch over our children. Everyone in the neighbourhood knew each other, just like back home in Greece.

Slowly, however, the years passed and our neighbourhood changed. Some people died, others sold their homes and went to live in other areas. The children that played chasey and hide and seek, grew up. They now go to the park with their boyfriends and girlfriends. But let me get back to the story I was telling.

Once we'd paid off this house that brought such initial sadness and so many joys as well, we saw that the children had grown and that it no longer fitted us. I remember that my Eleni used to sleep on the couch and when we had guests she had to wait till they had all left to go to sleep. George decided to knock the house down and build a large house given that the allotment was big enough, that we liked the area, it was close to the school, to transport, the shops, everything was close by and to our liking and so we made the decision.

Now I see that this decision was wrong. It was a very bad decision to demolish the toil of so many years and to start all over again. We should have rented it out and built our new house next to it. As I said, the allotment was large. Where the garden, the swings, the huge garage were, we should have built our new house as there was room to do so. Of course, these thoughts don't help anything now as they are all in hindsight. Back then we thought differently. We rented further down, knocked down our house and built a new, brick, large home, rather high, with seven steps leading up to it. During that period of time, George was a councillor in the local Council, and knew that the law did not allow the building of a two-storey house, our luck ran out. These days, I notice that all the blocks of land and all the little houses are transformed into two-storey dwellings. The laws have changed ...

Many happy events were celebrated in this house, birthdays, engagements, weddings. Our children have children, we have grandchildren. We had ten grandchildren but Fate grew envious of us and we lost our darling George, a young man of 19, in a car accident. He didn't get to enjoy young love, his youth, nothing at all, all were erased by a speeding car. I feel that I aged since then, that sorrow has taken root inside me, and no matter how I try to combat this feeling, it is always there.

Our neighbourhood

I live in Northcote and, at the time of writing my story, it is certain that this is where I will remain. I like it here and I have become one with the people and the place. It is a lovely area, with its shops, its parks, it has fine roads, good transport, schools, churches, anything that a person needs to live well. And I have so, so many memories here. All round me are friends and relatives, things that move me, pretty houses, small romantic parks, years of work, toil and dreams. Back then when we all dreamt of getting rich. At one stage, I worked for a Jewish boss. A wonderful man, serious in his demeanour, beautifully spoken, courteous and kind-hearted. He sent his son to his homeland to serve in the army. The rest of us couldn't understand his thinking in sending his son to the firing line. His name was Abraham and he would come in, here and there, to check on the state of affairs. He had a man named Jim to run things day to day. Jim was nice as well, a quiet man, but a bit of a flirt. Apparently he had remarried, but here in the factory he had a young girlfriend called Helen. Oh those infamous Helens! And I would observe him, noticing his protruding belly and, given that he was not handsome, was amazed at the young girl's choice. How could she go out with Jim? It's money, you see, that helps in these situations. Money helps in keeping this young woman running to her lover with the fat purse.

Another time, the children were little, two at school and one I'd take in the pram to be looked after by a local grandmother. I would hurriedly leave for work, hearing my baby's cries up until the corner where I'd turn and walk on …

I had good neighbours. The Dadons who had four children, poor people, polite, they reminded me of my parents and our poverty-stricken neighbours back home. Mrs Dadon would often ask for a lend of some money as times were hard for them. And I would think back to my own experiences in Greece, I had also lived through this nightmare, the nightmare of deprivation. One day her eldest son, Vroger, was yelling, spoiling the quiet of a Spring Day. He was young and had an empty stomach, he wanted food and, with the rage of youth, was demanding that his mother give him something to eat, without stopping to think whether she had anything to give him. His mother came to my door looking sad and embarrassed, asking for a couple of potatoes for her child. That day it just happened that I didn't have anything and I, thoughtlessly, quickly replied, 'Sorry, I don't have any.' And the woman turned and left. Later I thought about it and got very upset. I still feel guilty about this incident to this day. Why didn't I just run to the corner milkbar and buy two potatoes? Vroger reminded me of my brother Thano who would also yell and never made peace with the situation he found himself in.

And there on the corner of Northcote and Mitchell streets we had the Jordan family, religious, quiet people with eight children. Despite the poverty that beset them, we never heard a cry, a complaint or some form of exasperation from any of them. Surrounded by so many children, sometimes hungry, sometimes full, always sleepy because with so many children they didn't even get enough sleep. Their house was small, humble but pretty, with the fireplace always burning and a saucepan always on the fire. They didn't have beds for all the children. Yet they always went to school well-dressed, reminding me of my childhood days. Their house was always happy, the children clean and all of them had a pallid smile on their face. In spite of it all, I mean the poverty and privations, they lived a happy life.

I remember once being invited to a party that they threw at their home for their neighbours. The theme was that everyone had to go wearing a hat. All of us wore a hat. I always had a passion for hats and so this was a great opportunity. I bought a hat, put on my finest, and off I went. Do you want to know what happened? We all had a wonderful time and I won the prize for the best hat!

The neighbourhood children all got on very well and played out in the street together. There weren't many cars in those days, one here and there, and so there was no fear of them. They played, carefree, the same games that we played back in our homeland: hide and seek, hopscotch, they told each other stories, sang songs, and anything else they could think of. Beautiful, unforgettable years in our neighbourhood. Now the children have scattered like the birds.

Opposite me was grandma Thompson who had one daughter married to a Cypriot man named Niko. Her daughter had a child, James, from her first marriage, a beautiful, blue-eyed blonde boy who always looked sad. Nikos was a stern type and always seemed to have airs. Perhaps the presence of her son annoyed him. He always tried to convince us that he was different, someone important, a cut above the rest. But everyone in the neighbourhood knew that he hit the child, didn't want him around, saw him as an intruder to his married life, perhaps he was even jealous of the boy. He never let him play with the other children, telling him that he had to work selling newspapers and look after the dogs. He had a lot of dogs that he raced.

We had Margaret who was short, pretty, always busy running around and so vivacious that the fences creaked when she walked through the neighbourhood. Now she's just a little blob in some aged care facility. Her children are all married and she has grandchildren from mixed marriages. One of her daughters, Suzie, who was friends with my Eleni, married a Frenchman, and has a lovely family. All her children have done well. Sometimes they stop and consider that they have a mother, a grandmother. 'We just don't have time to go and see her.' Perhaps when they find the time to go and visit her it will be too late.

Further down, the McDonald family had three children that were a little older than the other children in the neighbourhood so they didn't keep company with the rest. Very courteous people, beautiful family, when the father passed away we went to the funeral and it was like a celebration. Each of his children talked about some event in their life and then they all sang together a song that their father liked very much and that they often sang when he was alive.

There were relatives of the Daltons from England who had three children and who also wrestled with poverty. One day they sold their house and returned to England. And there were the Constances who had a son, Ricki, who was a very innocent child. The mother would spend all evening at the pub and when you bumped into her she would sway as she walked, trying to find her balance. The kindly father was always working with a smile on his face and dressed like a star. And opposite, in the last house, there lived an Italian family whose children were also friends with mine. Their mother was always ill, and when I would pop in to see her and take her something, she would always complain about her other half and his womanising ways which were the reason for her being bedridden.

I nearly forgot about the strange couple. They were always fighting and then making up, an elderly couple without children, with a lovely cat for company. At the break of dawn, the elderly woman would sing out to her cat, 'tourlou tourlou', and even though she was a very old lady she had such a strong voice. My God, she was the alarm bell of the neighbourhood.

We move around within Northcote as the schools, the church, the shops are all close by. We all shop locally and I make an effort to interact. I stop by gardens with flowers to hear a 'good morning' from someone as this reminds me of the days when my children were little and those days when I lived in my beloved homeland. Some say that Northcote is a working-class suburb, that it isn't an aristocratic area with villas, limousines and wealthy women who have forgotten where they came from. They say that poor people live in Northcote. I always tell them that it is a very beautiful suburb, that the people have fine sentiments, and that the children can play freely around the neighbourhood. We have a beautiful park, and when I go for a walk under the trees my footsteps make a strange sound as they sink into the fallen leaves. This keeps me company and a feeling of pins and needles overwhelms me.

Northcote is good for those of us living here. Our children grew up here in Northcote, they married and have left for other suburbs. We are tied to this place. We feel a deep affinity with this place of our migration, we worked hard, we dreamed and are now living our dreams.

I remember when the children were young and we'd go on short trips or journeys away, upon returning as soon as we neared Northcote the children would yell, laughing happily, 'There it is, there it is, our little Northcote!'

Now we write stories, poems, books, we go to the Northcote Town Hall to launch them, and people say to us, 'Good on you for managing to write our stories.'

Living out my days

Saturday night and George and I came home from the theatre feeling happy with each other, a feeling of love for each other which was a rare sensation for us. I was especially happy because I managed to convince George to come to the theatre with me. I made him a cup of coffee and then said goodnight as I was going to bed. I felt so incredibly satisfied … my soul, my body was overflowing with a strong feeling of abundance, joy to spare, full of gratitude and I kept whispering endless 'thank yous'. I was thinking how wonderful it would be to live these sorts of moments more often … and, happy as I was, fell into a sweet sleep. At daybreak, I think it was around five in the morning, the phone rang and George answered it. My mind went to Greece, to our brothers and sisters there, as they usually rang at this time. In seconds our world was ruined. George came into my room, turned on the light.

'Litsa, get up, our George was in a car accident and is in hospital! Get up, let's go!'

From this moment began our Golgotha. We get to the hospital. Our boy was in surgery for about three to four hours and all of us, parents, grandparents, brothers, sisters, uncles, aunties, friends, two rooms full of people crying hysterically, in utter despair, anxious and, here and there, a secret hope that our child would pull through. But nothing, death took him. The messengers came and announced the fateful news. They were not able to save our boy, the excessive haemorrhaging was the end of our grandson.

I can't cope with this, I can't believe that he isn't going to come here to my house, to his bed. How are we going to endure such sorrow? And go on living?

What is it to be human? How do humans function and exist? I can't explain it. After so much devastation, such grief at losing our grandson, our beautiful young man, just nineteen years old, gone never to see him again, how do we survive this? How do people cope with death?

Our George has left us. I look at his photograph and I can't understand how it can be that he's gone, that we're never going to see him again. I search for him, for his forehead, his brow, his cheeks, his proud stance, I sit and chat with him and I wait for him. What am I waiting for? When I know that we put our child deep in that hole, that we covered him with thousands of flowers, and then at the wake we ate and drank, we talked with our respective group of friends while this child, our young grandson, was deep in the ground.

How do people endure this, his mother, his father, his brothers and sisters, his cousins, friends, everyone. He was loved by everyone because he was a good boy, polite, kind, always smiling, he had an angelic countenance, beautiful looking, as though formed by angels, he was everyone's favourite. How am I going to get through this? I had him here, in my house. He often slept over, now everything is silent, the house is falling all around me, I don't hear his footsteps, his voice, he doesn't come and lean over to kiss me. Although we tasted every kind of bitterness after losing him, what I truly don't understand is how we, I, get up and have a shower, dry myself with the towel, comb my hair, drink my coffee and continue on with my writing, with my daily responsibilities. How do I manage it? I don't know, it's impossible to comprehend. When friends and family came over to offer their condolences, what gave me the courage to talk about the car accident in detail? How do I continue to think about these things? The phone call, the early morning hours, the wait in the hospital, those traumatic hours when we anxiously awaited news about our child, and then came the end, no hope for him. They didn't even let us see him. Only his parents and his siblings.

How did they survive this? How do they continue to live! How do we all continue to live. Well, you might say that it's just our turn to drink the hemlock. We drank this poison, we still drink it and we will drink it for as long as we live. Despite all of this sorrow, we continue to live, we see the sun, we witness nature. I go to the verandah to hang out the washing and I am happy that I am able to see. Wherever my eyes turn, I think that I will see our boy, our grandson, our beloved George. I look at the photographs and can't believe that I am not going to see our fine young man again.

How bitter life is! Why such distress, such pain for us human beings! Everyone tells me to take courage, to give advice to his mother, to his father, his siblings. How can I when I, myself, am so devastated? My insides are bleeding, bitter. What sorrow and outrage is this, that death takes our handsome young men! My precious child was just 19-years-old. He didn't get a chance to live, to taste life, to blossom, when Hades took him from us. I walk around the house, waiting to hear his footsteps, his movement, bending over to kiss me like he used to. Now my grandson is no more, doesn't exist, is in that cemetery, buried in a deep hole.

George goes there every morning. I go here and there, even though he begs me to go with him. Today when he saw that I was particularly down, he said,

'Come on, let's go and pick some flowers from the garden and take them to our grandson.'

'No', I said, 'I don't want to, I can't, what you're doing doesn't help with anything. Do you think our young boy can see you, hear you?'

'Come on, let's go, perhaps he can see us, come on, it's good for us to go, maybe it's good for me, please come with me.'

'If this did any good I would give my life in exchange for his, to bring our child back to life. I would die happy.'

'Let's go, perhaps he can hear us, who knows?'

'No, he can't hear us, he can't see us … I wish I could give my life so he could live again … I would go happily to Hades.'

'You're going to go to Hades when it's your turn to go, for now let's go to the cemetery.'

'No. What does going back and forth to the cemetery achieve?'

Oh if only I could go instead, I would die an ecstatic woman!

'Let me be, please, let me be …'

And yet, even though I know there is no hope, even though I well know that I am never going to see again my cherished, my gentle grandson, and despite this pain, look at what strange animals we human beings are. I live out my days. I get up, I wash, I carry out my chores, I eat, I talk, I exist. Now, how I function, I really don't know, like a robot, some other force winds me up and I move around with this unbearable pain, without our beloved George.

I can't bear your loss
your absence is a piercing arrow
blood flows all around me.
There is a knock at the door
and I anticipate
you standing there.
The bed is empty
I sit there and caress it
like every Sunday.
Your grandfather consoles himself
he says, our George is an angel now,
he masks his sorrow.
Your grave is a pain in the soul
a garden with many colours
My George, you are a seed in the earth.
When I am drowning
I hear your voice
and emerge from the labyrinth.

The years have passed...

The years passed with much toil, difficult jobs, with rude comments from the locals, and with all the daily challenges that beset any life, even the most ordinary. But just imagine how many challenges our life presented us with as migrants, without any assistance, we didn't even know the language.

And here we are now, able to go back to the homeland that we held such nostalgia for all these years. Yet, when I returned to Greece, and to my place of birth, Aigion, after 35 years in a foreign land, nothing was the same as when I left it. Everything there seemed strange to me, small, inconsequential, where were the things I left? Most of my childhood friends and acquaintances had scattered here and there, the older people had died and most of the people around my age lived in other cities in Greece or abroad.

Everything was completely different now. Neither I nor they were the same people we once were, and our past life and our experiences back then didn't seem to matter at all to the people I now encountered. Moreover, it seemed to me that they had no interest in seeing us or hearing about our experiences as migrants living in another country. I, on the other hand, was interested in all of them and all things Greek. My childhood and youthful memories were still warm from those years, when I left for other parts, missing my homeland and my compatriots. The experience of migration fills you with nostalgia for everything you lived through and left behind. This is not the case amongst those left behind. And I say this because when I would reconnect with someone I knew, my heart felt like bursting from joy, so emotional was I about sharing what had happened to us during those 35 years apart. After the usual hugs and niceties that are the norm in such situations, there would fall a silence, a heaviness in the air that I still can't explain, standing there mute, disappointed before finally saying goodbye.

What happened to all those things you wanted to ask about your friends, your neighbours, about the life you missed out on during your endless struggle to survive your migration? And I have to wonder why time is so catastrophic in its passing for some people's relationships and the things they love.

I have made three trips to my homeland, in 1985, 1992 and 1996 but, unfortunately, I didn't experience what I was weaving in my mind for thirty years. When I'm in Australia I miss my friends with every fibre of my being and say, oh, the next time that I go to Greece, I'm definitely going to catch up with Parthena, Kiki, Giota, Athanasia, Lambi, Alexandra's son George, Vasilo's son Pano, Maro, Mrs Panagiotaina's son Thimio and so many others that I miss. But when I get to Greece, all these sensitivities that I nurse within my soul seem useless and unimportant.

I remember that one summer, I met with two of my girlfriends from past days. We ate, drank, talked for hours and about so many things, but nothing about the old days and about our separating when I left, about the things we had lived through. Time stood between us, ever-mighty, hateful and the victor. We said nothing about the war years, our poverty, our wretchedness or about the humble way we entertained ourselves after the war, the cinema, the beach days, the flirting, the small joys, nothing, nothing, nothing. They had forgotten everything. They had beautiful houses with expensive furniture, with luxurious bathrooms etc, with a holiday house, they had assumed a different manner to match and had forgotten everything while I thought back to the hovels they used to live in, the hunger and the desperation. They didn't say a word about the old days. Everything forgotten with time.

When I look back on the old days and recall scenes from my life, I have to say that I am content with the life I live now, because I have everything I need and can go for trips to Greece, whereas back then I had no money not only for trips but to even buy a pencil. I have to say that I always got on well with my adopted homeland, my stepmother, I feel good here, and that only the indifference of my compatriots back home sometimes hurts me, but never mind. If I can, I'd like to visit my homeland again because I love her and keep her as a talisman so that I can better live the days of my migration.

For the children of migrants

Five-year-old child home from school, but nobody had time to keep him company, because everyone was busy in the front shop. People got home from work and would go to the shop for numerous provisions, back in the day when Milk Bars were at the height of their popularity. It was extremely busy at that hour when workers were returning home. We didn't have time even to scratch ourselves, let alone look after a child, we couldn't see in front of us we were running around so much.

Within this chaos, the little boy snuck down to the back of the shop and went to the storeroom to find something to play with. He wanted company and found it. He started opening the cans of coca cola and enjoyed the patterns that the froth made as it spurted into the air. His face shone from excitement.

As soon as the work eased off a bit, the mother went to find her little boy to give him some milk, to look after him, to hug him, and to rest from the rigours of the day.

She found her child soaked through and surrounded by empty coca cola cans. The father got so angry, his rage fuelled by the waste and his own exhaustion, that he went to hit the child. The mother threw herself between them, the little one ran into her arms, and everything calmed down. The mother, being by nature a peacemaker, calmed her husband down by using logic and convincing him that the child wasn't to blame for what occurred.

Another afternoon, while the parents were focused on the rush hour in the shop with people buying goods before going home, there were no supermarkets in those days, in this flurry of activity their little boy slipped outside without the parents noticing.

When the last customer had gone, the mother went to the room where everything in their life revolved, a room that had many titles – loungeroom, dining room, kitchen, storeroom – to be with her child. She had left him there playing with a little toy car. But she couldn't see him anywhere. The mother started to get worried. She ventured towards the back of the shop to the laundry, went out into the backyard that was overgrown with long grass, the sight of which brought sadness. But who had time to look after and maintain a garden!

Nothing. She couldn't see her son anywhere. She ran back to the shop visibly agitated, saying to her husband, 'I can't find him anywhere, what's happened to our child?' They ran to the front of the shop and asked the neighbours. No one had seen him all afternoon.

They rang the police, anxious that something sinister had happened. Someone kidnapped their child when they were knee deep in work serving their customers. Their frenzied worry made them forget how to behave. They were hysterical, running in all directions, two bodies desperately trying to find out some news.

They want their child. The mother pleads, she wants her precious child. How did he disappear like that? She mumbles blessings, 'Please, my child, where are you, I will never tell you off again, I will never let you out of my sight again, I will tell your father that I can't help him in the shop anymore … I will stay with you, take you for a walk to the park, please come back and you'll see.'

The father, devastated, tries to remain strong, brave and hopeful so that he can continue serving the customers that walked into the shop unaware of what was going on.

And this is what happened. During this busy time of day, a customer left his car outside the shop, came in, organised his purchases, exchanged a few words with the child's father, took his things, got in his car, started the car engine and off he went.

Unbeknown to the driver, when he was inside, the child slid out of the front door of the shop, got in the car, and lied down in the back seat, enjoying the experience as his parents didn't have a car.

When the man reached his home, he parked his car, took his shopping and that's when he noticed that a little boy he used to see at the Milk Bar was lying in the back seat. He immediately understood what had happened, got in the car again and returned the child.

I will never forget that extraordinary moment when I saw the man come into the shop, holding my child by the hand. I wish this man well, wherever he may be, and thank him for the great joy that he brought to my life that day when I felt that all was lost.

I don't think that my child quite understood what happened that afternoon and how worried we became. He actually looked quite happy to have gone on a trip in a car! But when things calmed down, we talked to him about never doing anything like that again and assured him that we would soon be buying our own car and going for drives.

There were so many things that happened, I don't know where to start. How could I ever forget one particular mother back then who lived through the most tragic experience of all of us.

When we grew tired of this way of life, the endless working hours, the upheaval, and the absence of any sort of recreation, we decided to rent the shop out, return to our home and start working nine to five again. When all is said and done, working for weekly wages means less stress. It means you can have a more normal life even if you do earn less. Of course, the shop earnings were better but we were exhausted, we did all we could do, let others have a go. I'm saying all this for the benefit of those who don't know what it's like to run a small business. Those who have been involved in such businesses know the endless hours you have to front up there, whether you feel well or not, carrying out your duties and waiting for the next customer.

Anyway, everything was organised, and we rented the shop we had in Footscray to a couple with two small children. They entered the fray in the hope of something better since the shop also had a house in the back. They seemed happy about this move. But none of us knows what life has in store for us at the dawn of each day.

One day, this woman put a pot with water on to boil to make some spaghetti when the bell rang that she needed to get back to the shop to help her husband. In her haste, she didn't notice that the handle of the pot was sticking out, neither did she think to take her child with her. She absentmindedly left the child playing dejectedly in the corner as, at that moment, the shop was very busy.

The child, on the other hand, looking around for its mother and not seeing her next to the stove, noticed the coloured lights of the gas when the water started to boil over. The little one drew near, got on her tip toes, looking intently at this brightly-lit game. She stretched out her little hand, grabbed hold of the handle and, in an instant, all that boiling water fell onto this tender angel making her scream hysterically.

As soon as the mother heard the screams she felt as though struck by lightning as to what might have happened in the kitchen. She ran inside and what did she see? Her precious angel on the floor with her face disfigured, writhing in pain. She grabbed hold of the child and the torturous struggle began. Mother and child ran to the hospital. The doctors gave hope in one instant that the worst was over, only to dash her hopes the next. The mother became unrecognisable within hours and she felt like she was living her worst nightmare. With the little strength she had left, she tried to imagine her child as she once was, a healthy, beautiful little girl. How was it possible that she was seeing a disfigured creature, her angel in so much pain … No, it was not possible. This must be a nightmare. And yet it wasn't a nightmare. She was in a hospital living this tragedy.

A doctor and nurse came to talk to her, gave her a glass of water, with the doctor looking at her kindly, trying to find the courage to tell her what needed to be said. He took her arm and said that she must be strong and that perhaps it's for the best that the child had died and was no longer suffering. Her face was so badly burnt that her life would be unendurable.

Now, how this mother accepted this news, only she knows. Only her heart knows how she lived and continues to live with the guilt that she, herself, caused the death of her child. And yet she lived through these tragic circumstances and everything was organised according to the required rituals: the flowers, the funeral, the announcements, the condolences, the embraces, the kisses of comfort, the handshakes and then nothing, just … nothing. And this poor, wretched woman having to go on talking, getting dressed, eating, serving her customers, finding the strength to smile, to do her housework, all the while living where the tragedy took place. How did she survive this life sentence? They had signed a contract for the business and couldn't abandon it, they had to survive. Who could possibly understand what horror they were living through?

Her husband tried to get her to forget, telling her that they would have other children. Really, how different men are to women?

Whenever I'd visit to comfort her, to keep her company, oh how I felt for her, seeing her drift around the house so devastated and defeated, a lifeless body, her every movement insurmountably difficult.

The years slowly passed, they left the shop, that place that had poisoned her breath and very being. I lost trace of her. Perhaps she was trying to forget and wanted no reminders of the past. I hope she is well and that time healed her pain, although I don't think that anything heals that sort of pain for a mother who lost her child under such circumstances.

Yes, migrant mothers and their children suffered things that can't be healed.

Where do I start in recounting the drama that our children lived through? The parents at the factory, one working the day shift, the other the afternoon shift to enable them to look after the children, but the hours never worked out and the children were left at home alone for a few hours till the mother returned from the factory.

The older son is four-years old and the little girl is two; the big brother is responsible for the younger child. Before the father left for work, he got everything ready in the front room, looked at this child, the little Petros, intently in the eyes, put his hand on his shoulder as though talking to a much older child and said, 'Be careful, my boy, and never forget what I am about to tell you: don't open the door to anyone until you see your mother, through the window, coming towards you. She won't be long. She'll be home soon.'

He kissed his children and left. He locked the door behind him and went to earn his daily bread. The weight of responsibility that little boy felt in having to watch over his little sister made him feel older than his years.

He now recalls those days and sees himself glued to the window watching the movement outside. This passing movement of life gave him courage and made him feel less alone with his little sister. What gave him courage, together with joy and sadness, was the Mr Whippy van, an ice-cream seller that passed by the house on summer days. He would hear the familiar, loud tune playing that signalled Mr Whippy's arrival, would see the brightly coloured vehicle, and he couldn't go outside to buy ice-cream. Oh! How he longed to buy one too, for himself and his little sister, one of those ice-creams in a cone, to hold it in his tiny hand, one of those with pink, white and chocolate colours! Yes, that was the one he wanted. He liked all the flavours, but getting one was impossible. He would try to feel better by saying that it didn't matter as he didn't want any ice-cream anyway, but he hoped that the multi-coloured van that parked outside his window would not leave before his mother came home. It had become his beloved friend, a sort of cheery companion.

Now that Petros is married with children of his own and his wife doesn't need to leave them anywhere to go to work, his mother was once showing me a family photograph. She started tearing and let out a deep sigh, saying, 'I have a soft spot for this child because he is a tortured soul, growing up before his time, always responsible for his brothers and sisters. He never played in a carefree way, he had no toys like his children do, I think his inner world was affected, and that's why he's always quiet, deep in thought. Perhaps the shadows of his childhood years continue to haunt him. I always try to do my best by this boy, I want to see him happy but I never quite manage it, he's always somewhere in the distant past.'

Our children had a rough time of it, never able to just be children. Us adults found ourselves in a foreign land, we were poor and running to work in the factories where they called us 'bloody wogs', which was the exact same slur that our children heard in school causing their little hearts to bleed. As soon as these children came home from school, they would throw their bags inside and go straight into the shop so that the mother could go inside to cook, to wash, to do the housework, the basic chores, because most of us back then ran Milk Bars.

I remember that one day I went to visit an acquaintance of mine who was working in a shop. Her older children were at school and she had placed her little one in a box for safety reasons. At the time that I went, the shop was very busy, full of customers, and inside the child was screaming and crying.

I went inside to see what was wrong. The poor little thing had soiled itself, snot was hanging from its nose, tears were streaming down its face, and it was licking this mixture, all the while screaming as though being killed. It seemed to be crying mostly from being confined to the box and not managing to get out. As soon as I grabbed it up into my arms and tended to its needs, it calmed down and looked at me intently as though trying to say 'thank you'.

How much our children suffered! I remember when our children were to go on a school excursion and brought the form home for us to sign if either one of us parents would like to accompany them and I remember that I never managed to go because the debt was such that we couldn't lose a day's pay. It was out of the question.

But our children needed this. They wanted us to accompany them sometimes, just like the Australian mothers managed to do, and they criticised us for not following suit. Our children hurt inside. They found themselves in two distinct worlds. At school with the English language and the Australian way of life, which was only logical, and then with us, the parents, the Greek patriots, insisting that the minute the children set foot in the door that they shed their skin like snakes do, and become Greek children. Our children were tired from school all day and we would grab them and take them to the Greek schools to learn Greek.

Oh, my children, you faced your own Golgotha which was very complex, difficult and painful. You wavered between two different confusing states and you really struggled to find some sort of balance but you are wonderful, you progressed and became good people and you deserve much praise. As for us, your parents, we apologise if we caused you stress, if we ever upset you, if we were unable to offer you the things that every child wants when they're little: to feel carefree and happy in their childhood world. I am certain, though, that your own children will be able to live as every child should.

There's some justification for our actions because our generation struggled in this foreign land, denied the time to focus as much as we should have on our children. Because we had suffered and lacked the basics in life, we tried to ensure that our children never went without food, cake, chocolate, a bed with clean sheets, and when we'd provided all of that, we thought we had done our duty. Since our children had all the material possessions that we never had growing up, we thought that they would be happy. We didn't think, or rather we didn't have time to think, about the internal world of our children. We didn't think to ask them how they felt, if they were happy about seeing the Australian children going on excursions with their parents, going together to Luna Park, to the zoo, to the football, on trips away during the school holidays to enjoy nature. These things were pushed aside.

Our children, children of migrant parents, of our generation went without so much and we have to acknowledge that. We were chasing after the dollar, there was no time to devote to our children who needed us so much, whose hearts ached at hearing the Australian children talk about how they spent their holidays during 'show and tell'.

It is important to record these things so that our children, and others, know how hard our life was, the life of a migrant who tried to establish a family, a property, without any support.

My dear, long-suffering children, you too had to partake of exile's bitterness. You also experienced the problems of migration.

A breakfast outing at 80

The day that I turned eighty, my granddaughters Bianca and Juliana came and we all went out for breakfast. This was a first for me.

They took me to a modern café in the city, which seemed to me to be a place where young people meet as it had thick wooden tables and stools instead of chairs. The waitresses wore clothes from the 1950s and didn't look like current young girls. As soon as we sat and my granddaughters ordered what we liked, they started asking me questions.

'Yiayia, what do you think, do you like it here?'

'It's lovely, really beautiful. Everything is fine it's just that I'm not used to such splendour.'

'Oh Yiayia, today you must be so happy because it is a special day for you. You're eighty and, you know what, you don't look it at all and you do so many interesting things. We're proud that you're our grandmother.'

'May you always keep well, my children, may you be healthy and do well in life and always think of others, love those around you and whenever you can, do things for other people less fortunate.'

Chatting away, we finished our breakfast and a waitress came to take our plates, Bianca paid the bill and we left. As soon as we got in the car, the girls turned to me and said that we would be going to a shop where I could buy whatever I needed for my painting given how much I enjoyed it. Bianca and Julia had seen an exercise book where I had done pencil drawings of objects from a book given to me by my nephew Mihalis, my sister Athina's son. Mihalis is a talented artist and whenever anyone sees his works they always praise them highly. Mihalis is the one who talked to me and showed me some things about art. Anyway, they took me to a shop that had anything an artist could wish for. I bought whatever I thought I might need and, indeed, I was very lucky because I found a small easel that you can sit on top of a table so it doesn't take up too much room. I have now placed it on a piece of furniture next to a window, which really suits me. The girls were so excited and kept asking me if I was happy. I was very, very happy, especially because we spent such a wonderful day altogether, a day I will never forget. There was joy and kisses and the girls left for Geelong, where they live. And there's me, Litsa, like a small child, opening the box of paints and all the other things as if they were a New Year's present.

George was watching me, laughed and said a little ironically,

'What can I say, it seems strange to me that you want to draw now in your old age.'

'Why do you find it funny? I like doing this, you'll see.'

I slowly started painting flowers. My grandchildren love them and every time they come for a visit, they are so happy to choose one of my works to take home with them. I'm even more happy than the children. I paint enthusiastically and a good friend of mine, who is interested in fine arts, said that she would organise an exhibition of my works in her house.

Epilogue: journey to the homeland

The days flowed quietly by, as though I were swimming in a lake and I was floating in calmness. I didn't know what to admire first, all these forgotten sights I now had before me, treasures of a beautiful landscape.

In the mornings I would walk along the pathways that led me to our vineyard and I felt the coolness like a balm entering the pores of my skin.

What an exultant moment for migrants, to find themselves in their homeland, after so much hard work and deprivation toiling for a daily wage in a foreign land!

I lean over the still waters that welcome me with the rhythm of their song and I feel as though reborn.

What a mystery they are, these abundant beauties of my homeland. As you encounter all of these Greek sights, our sights, our precious sights, that have been sung about countless times, that have been glorified, that cloak me in a garment of gossamer, these envied sights that indulge me to the point of intoxication, tranquil song, that heals the pain of the migrant.

The morning's gentle breeze, music to the senses, accompanies my past life, the season of youth, of war, followed by the decision to migrate for a daily paypacket, for clothes on our back, for a bite to eat and for our self-respect.

Yes, all of these daggers encircle me, keep me company, bewitch me, tie me to this land where I was born, where I suffered deprivations. Strong, inexplicable emotions that make me feel proud of the country where my parents are laid to rest.

About the Translator

Konstandina Dounis (BA, DipEd, MLitt, MA, PhD) is an award-winning academic, author and literary translator. She is the recipient of the Monash University MSA Award for Teaching Excellence 2018; AALITRA Award for Literary Translation 2020, 2nd Prize; GACL Literary Competition Prose 2020, 1st Prize. She has published widely – both in terms of scholarly articles, literary translations and monographs – on the Greek Diaspora, women's writing and the complexities of historical recordings within the framework of migration. Recent published translations include: Dina Amanatides, *Dreams of Clay, Drops of Dew*; George Zangalis, *An Ode to Mother, to my Mother, the Other Eleni;* Ekaterini Mpaloukas, *The Widows and the Dear Departed;* Nikos Ninolakis, *On the Ship of Dreams.*

www.ingramcontent.com/pod-product-compliance
Ingram Content Group Australia Pty Ltd
76 Discovery Rd, Dandenong South VIC 3175, AU
AUHW020135130726
429791AU00003B/118

9 781922 669506